MW00647123

"This is IT finally, a refreshing real book disc
this book actually sees sex as a relational dar
book is easy to read and goes beyond form
empathy which so often are missing in so-ca...... ... . This is where the field of
sex therapy needs to go. The lovers in this book tell us how we often settle for being
stuck in clichés and so-called symptoms and miss the symphony that great sex can be."
— **Sue Johnson, Ed.D.**, researcher, professor and bestselling author
of Hold me tight: Seven conversations for a lifetime of love

"With empirical rigor and a playful sense of humor, Kleinplatz and Ménard offer us
a grand tour of a previously undocumented world where extraordinary lovers create
magnificent sexual experiences. Every sex therapist, educator, researcher and student
should read this book. It will utterly transform the conversation around sexual desire."
— **Emily Nagoski, Ph.D.**, author of *Come as you are: The surprising
new science that will transform your sex life*

"This is a wonderful book! Taking the focus off of 'sex' and 'sexual function' tricks and
techniques, it will provide an invaluable resource for those looking to truly improve
the quality of their relationships and their experience of sex."
— **Daniel N. Watter, Ed.D.**, Past President, The Society
for Sex Therapy and Research (SSTAR)

"Peggy Kleinplatz has achieved near mythical status in the echelons of sex therapy.
For nearly two decades she has been leading the Optimal Sexual Experiences Research
Team at the University of Ottawa and carefully protecting their work from outside
eyes. Along the way, they have teased and tantalized us with breadcrumbs of insight
from their detailed study of actual couples who embody and manifest the eight
components of magnificent sex; but now, finally, Kleinplatz and Ménard have given us
the secret sauce, and it was worth the wait!"
— **Ian Kerner, Ph.D., LMFT**, *New York Times* best-selling
author, *She comes first*

"Would you like to have good sex? What about great sex? Or, even better, what about
the greatest sexual experience of your life? Kleinplatz and Ménard dive into their
incredible research on peak sexual experiences, and distill valuable lessons to help you
to discover your potential for sexual ecstasy. This isn't a cookbook style sex manual – it's
a guide to creating sexual authenticity in your life, in a way that translates into heights
of sexual fulfillment."
— **David Ley, Ph.D.**, licensed clinical psychologist
and AASECT Certified Sex Therapist & Supervisor

"Kleinplatz and Ménard have conducted extensive research on optimal sex and this
book beautifully illustrates their work. It offers intimate details in selected quotes as
described by their sexually-gratified subjects. *Magnificent Sex: Lessons from Extraordinary
Lovers* will be of great value to readers in the general public as well as to those in the
related fields of sexuality science, education and therapy."
— **Stella Resnick, Ph.D.**, sex therapist and author of *Body-to-body intimacy:
Transformation through love, sex and neurobiology*

"Kleinplatz and Ménard investigate sex in the great tradition of Abraham Maslow and the humanistic tradition, as well as the more recent trend of positive psychology, which shift the focus from human dysfunction to human flourishing. While much time and resources have been invested in the study of how sex goes wrong and how to shift from abnormal or dysfunctional sex to functional sex, this book places the emphasis on how couples can set to work to achieve higher and higher levels of sexual pleasure and intimacy. Grounded in empirical science that aims and succeeds at respecting the fidelity of lived sexual experience, this book offers hope for individuals and couples that great sex need not remain restricted to the realm of fantasy."

— **Brent Dean Robbins, Ph.D.**, chair and professor of psychology at Point Park University and author of *The medicalized body and anesthetic culture: The cadaver, the memorial body, and the recovery of lived experience*

"Magnificent sex! It's something many crave, but too few have. It's also a phenomenon that looks nothing like the false media images perpetuating it. In this compelling book, full of striking quotes from real people having superb sex, the authors paint a picture of what truly great sex looks like. Using results from their in-depth study of people having magnificent sex, they reveal the personal and relationship qualities and attitudes necessary for magnificent sex. Unlike books promising results in a few simple steps, this book will shift our paradigm of great sex – and help guide our way there."

— **Laurie Mintz, Ph.D.**, professor at the University of Florida and author of *A tired woman's guide to passionate sex* and *Becoming cliterate: Why orgasm equality matters – and how to get it*

"*Magnificent Sex* is a much-needed alternative to the hundreds of books about amping up your sex life that amount to cookbooks of positions and toys. Instead, Kleinplatz and Ménard have researched actual couples who still manage to have exceptional sex after years of marriage, and distilled their secrets and wisdom. The couples they interviewed represent a broad range of diversity, and the insights are unexpected – they are all about attitude and perspective, and have little to do with mechanics. This book is destined to become a classic. It is a book for therapists, but also for anyone who is hoping to keep the spark of passion alive in their relationship."

— **Margaret Nichols, Ph.D.**, psychologist and AASECT certified sex therapy supervisor, Institute for Personal Growth, Highland Park, Jersey City, and Freehold New Jersey

"This book is both original and effective in providing a guide to quality sex in a manner supported by research and avoidance of hyperbole. A valuable read that adds to our knowledge of the entire spectrum of sexualities, from dysfunctional to 'normal' to optimal!"

— **Michael A. Perelman, Ph.D.**, co-director, Human Sexuality Program, Weill Cornell Medicine, New York-Presbyterian

Magnificent Sex

What makes sex magnificent? What are the qualities of extraordinary erotic intimacy and what are the elements that help to bring it about? Is great sex the stuff that people remember nostalgically from the "honeymoon" phase of their relationships, or can sex improve over time?

Magnificent Sex is based on the largest, in-depth interview study ever conducted with people who are having extraordinary sex. It gathers the nuggets for remarkable sex from the "experts", distilling them into an attainable blueprint for ordinary lovers who want to make erotic intimacy grow over the course of a lifetime. Looking at factors including individual and relational qualities, empathic communication and the myths and realities of magnificent sex, this book offers accessible and evidence-based guidance for lovers and therapists alike.

It is replete with frank and often humorous interviews with straight and LGBTQ individuals and couples, those who are "vanilla" and "kinky", monogamous and consensually non-monogamous and healthy and chronically ill. This illuminating book explores the implications of the findings to develop a model that effectively tackles the common problems of low desire and frequency. The "cure" for low desire is to create desirable sex!

Peggy J. Kleinplatz, Ph.D., is Professor in the Faculty of Medicine and Director of Sex and Couples Therapy Training at the University of Ottawa, Canada. She was awarded the Prix d'Excellence in 2000 for her teaching of Human Sexuality. She is a Certified Sex Therapist and Educator. She is Director of the Optimal Sexual Experiences Research Team of the University of Ottawa and has a particular interest in sexual health in the elderly, disabled and marginalized populations. Please see optimalsexualexperiences.com. Kleinplatz has edited four books, notably *New Directions in Sex Therapy:*

Innovations and Alternatives (2012), winner of the AASECT 2013 Book Award, *Sadomasochism: Powerful Pleasures* with Charles Moser, Ph.D., M.D. (2006) and *Sexuality and Ageing* with Walter Bouman, M.D. (2015). In 2015, Kleinplatz received the American Association of Sexuality Educators, Counselors and Therapists' Professional Standard of Excellence Award.

A. Dana Ménard, Ph.D., is currently a clinical psychologist and adjunct professor in the Faculty of Science at the University of Windsor in Windsor, Ontario. She earned a Ph.D. in clinical psychology from the University of Ottawa in 2013, an M.A. in experimental psychology from Carleton University in 2007 and a B.Sc. in psychology from the University of Ottawa in 2005. She has held previous academic appointments at the University of Western Ontario and at Wayne State University in Detroit, Michigan. As a clinician, Dr. Ménard has worked at Detroit Receiving Hospital, the London Health Sciences Centre, the Royal Ottawa Hospital and the Ottawa Hospital, among others. Aside from her work on magnificent sex, she has also researched and published in the areas of sexuality in the media, adult survivors of child sexual abuse, student mental health and well-being and academic lab safety.

Magnificent Sex

Lessons from Extraordinary
Lovers

PEGGY J. KLEINPLATZ, PH.D.
A. DANA MÉNARD, PH.D.

Routledge
Taylor & Francis Group

NEW YORK AND LONDON

First published 2020
by Routledge
52 Vanderbilt Avenue, New York, NY 10017

and by Routledge
2 Park Square, Milton Park, Abingdon, Oxon, OX14 4RN

Routledge is an imprint of the Taylor & Francis Group, an informa business

Library of Congress Cataloging-in-Publication Data
A catalog record for this book has been requested

ISBN: 978-0-367-18136-9 (hbk)
ISBN: 978-0-367-18137-6 (pbk)
ISBN: 978-0-429-05968-1 (ebk)

Typeset in Avenir and Dante
by Apex CoVantage, LLC

This book is dedicated in memory of our fathers,
Mayer Kleinplatz and Daniel Ménard.
May their memories always be a blessing.

Contents

Acknowledgements

We would like to thank a number of people who have worked with us over the last 15 years to make this book possible. First and foremost, our most profound gratitude goes to our participants, who shared so deeply and so honestly with us about the best and worst moments of their lives. The contribution they have made to advancing the fields of sex research and sex therapy is immeasurable. The second group who made this research possible is the Optimal Sexual Experiences Research Team of the University of Ottawa, including both previous and current members. They helped us transform our participants' beautiful words into clear pathways up the mountain. Special thanks to Nicolas Paradis, M.Ed., Meghan Campbell, Psy.D., Shannon Lawless, M.S., Lianne Rosen, Ph.D., Maxime Charest, M.A., Marlene Neufeld, M.S.W., Robert Neufeld, M.Ed., Danielle Pratt, R.M.T., Bogdan Buduru, Ph.D., Myddryn Ellis, B.Sc., Diana L. Scamolla, B.A., and especially Jessica Lafreniere, B.A. who keeps us all on track with pure sunshine. Thank you all for your energy, your enthusiasm and your appreciation of adventure and discovery.

Thank you to the group therapy clients and to the teams of therapist-research collaborators who made it possible to answer the big questions: Can any old person have magnificent sex? For that matter, might any young person be capable of optimal erotic intimacy? We would not know that the answer to these bottom line questions is "Yes" if not for your courage, your willingness to share your experiences and to dream bigger.

Thanks to Routledge Senior Editor, Clare Ashworth, for her steady calm, demeanour combined with gentle encouragement and her eagle eye. Thanks also to the rest of the team at Routledge, especially to Production Editor Alison Macfarlane, for her attention to detail and generosity of spirit and time, and to Editorial Assistant Ellie Duncan and Copy Editor Sophie Rosinke. Ms. Rosinke was remarkably patient as we dealt with the technical nightmare of merging Canadian spelling, APA style and British punctuation.

Special thanks to Diana L. Scamolla, B.A., Maxime Charest, M.A., and Tricia Robinson for their assistance with and design of the illustrations.

Thanks to Barry McCarthy, Ph.D., Sue Johnson-Douglas, Ed.D. and Alexander Štulhofer, Ph.D. for their help and support in designing clinical trials for our current intervention.

Thanks to everyone who guided us through the sometimes intimidating process of getting this book published.

Peggy J. Kleinplatz would like to thank the late Alvin R. Mahrer, Ph.D. for literally writing the book – or rather, the two books – on optimal ways of being. He continues to inspire and guide all my work.

Thanks also to the special friends and family who have been there, supporting me every step along this path for many years.

I remain beholden to my beloved, who continues to illuminate the peaks for me despite the years since his passing.

Dana Ménard would like to thank former colleagues and supervisors from the University of Ottawa and the London Health Sciences Centre, and current colleagues at the University of Windsor. Special thanks to Isabelle and Claire, long-time friends who always shared my passion for sex research. Snuggles and pats for the four-legged friends who kept me company in the writing of this book. Finally, my deepest appreciation and love to my husband, John Trant, who has supported me every step of the way.

PART I

PART I

INTRODUCTION

How Did We Come to Be Studying Magnificent Sex?

I [P.J.K.] have been teaching human sexuality at the University of Ottawa and practising sex therapy for most of my life. One might think that sex therapists aim to improve patients' sex lives. To a certain extent, that is precisely what we do. We see clients who have symptoms of sexual dysfunctions (e.g., erectile dysfunction, difficulties with orgasm or pain on intercourse) and we help to alleviate their difficulties. Sex therapists are reasonably good at it. Unfortunately, though, that is about the extent of what we aim to do. We take people who have bad sex or painful sex and help them to function normally – whatever that means – so that they might have tolerable sex. We are rather limited in our goals. What are we to do about that most vexing of sexual problems, that is, low desire or low frequency of sex? Low sexual desire / frequency is defined as engaging in sex less than 12 times per year (McCarthy & McCarthy, 2020). It is the most common of the problems encountered in sex therapy and conventional treatment approaches have generally not proven to be effective in dealing with it (Leiblum, 2010).

The state of the art in sex therapy stands in rather stark contrast to what our "competitors" in popular culture would have us believe about sex. The media are filled with images of "great sex". Magazines and sex manuals are filled with tips, tricks and techniques for how to have mind-blowing sex. A quick google search will return millions of hits. Porn tends to make great sex look even easier. In fact, it looks utterly effortless. In the world of porn, all penises are hard; penetration requires no lube; a few thrusts are all a woman needs to be orgasmic; there are never interruptions, unless someone arrives for a threesome; and there is an absence of verbal communication, unless one counts moans and groans. Porn provides convincing and entertaining fiction, so captivating that it is easy to forget it is about as realistic as children's fairy tales. And just like fairy tales, it leaves us with the message that dreams can come true. (I have no problem with porn, except in so far as my patients and students mistake it for reality and judge themselves as unable to measure up.)

Which Way to Erotic Intimacy?

The link between the vestiges of erotic potential harboured by clients and the anticipation engendered by desirable sex became apparent in my sex therapy practice in the 1980s. In late 1989, three clients were referred to me in the course of one week, each diagnosed with what was then called Inhibited Sexual Desire (or simply, low desire) subsequent to a history of childhood sexual abuse. I had learned by then to ask clients routinely about their best sexual experiences rather than focusing only on their current problems. This turns out to be a particularly advantageous inquiry in dealing with low sexual desire (Kleinplatz, 2010). I asked these three clients to describe the incidents in their pasts when they had been filled with intense sexual longings. For people who have no recollection of ever having wanted sex, such a question may at first seem puzzling. Yet all three of these individuals were able to identify memories of powerful erotic desires, of wanting more . . . though more of what was not clear. Each had been an adolescent, making out while fully dressed. Each conceded there had been no genital contact, let alone "sex". If these individuals had felt their peak sexual desire had occurred while they were still virgins, it made me wonder what it means when we speak of "sexual" desire (Kleinplatz, 1992). In fact, it made me wonder what we mean by "sex". Why do people settle for lacklustre sex lives when they have had a glimpse of their dreams? What would the "best sex" look like, if people actually had the opportunity to experience it? These musings changed my clinical career and led me to focus on helping my clients to develop optimal erotic intimacy, regardless of past experiences. More importantly, they led me to wonder about why so many people think they ought to feel "sexual" desire in the absence of sex worth wanting (Kleinplatz, 1992, 2006, 2016).

It was another series of events that changed the trajectory of my research career. In 2004, I was teaching Human Sexuality and one of the undergraduate students kept asking questions that came out of reading *Glamour* and *Cosmo*. She would compare and contrast messages put forth by women's magazines with the studies she had heard about in my classes.

She wanted data about "great sex". That was how I came to meet A. Dana Ménard, then an undergraduate student, later to become A. Dana Ménard, Ph.D. She had a strong background in "hard" sciences and had already earned two scholarships to support her burgeoning career in bee research. It was perhaps her misfortune that one too many bee stings had led to an allergic reaction and my good fortune to begin working with her in studying optimal sexual experience.

In 2005, we began to study "great sex". But where might we gather knowledge on the kinds of sex worth wanting? It was in 2005 that we and the Optimal Sexual Experiences Research Team of the University of Ottawa began our series of studies on extraordinary lovers and how their experiences might inform average people – and ordinary sex therapists – who might want to aim higher. It is these studies and their implications for couples, for therapists and for sex itself that we plan to share in this book. In parallel to the optimal sexual experience studies, Dr. Ménard, then a graduate student, began a program of research examining the portrayal of sex, sexuality and romance in the media, ranging from advice columns to romance novels to slasher movies. She was quickly amassing the data that demonstrated how badly the public was being misinformed about sex (Cabrera & Ménard, 2012; Ménard & Cabrera, 2011; Ménard & Kleinplatz, 2008; Ménard, Weaver & Cabrera, 2019).

What Is the Plan of This Book and for Whom Is It Intended?

This book begins with an overview of our studies and will provide some background as to why we undertook them (Chapter 1). Although the fields of sex research in general and sex therapy in particular have amassed a great deal of information on bad or "dysfunctional" sex and average or "functional" sex, the literature on "great sex" or magnificent sex is close to non-existent. Our empirical work, we hope, will begin to change that. We then describe precisely how we undertook the research, recruited participants and which questions we asked to help us find meaningful and clinically useful answers. In short, in order to study optimal sexual experience, we needed data as to what "great sex" really is and how it resembled or differed from media depictions. The components or building blocks of magnificent sex are described in Chapter 2. Once we had empirical findings as to what constituted real-life, optimal erotic experience, we wanted to know what lessons extraordinary lovers might have to offer the rest of us (Chapter 3). In Chapter 3, we will contrast the reality of extraordinary erotic intimacy with media-driven, misleading ideas about "great sex". That is, we will expose and debunk the myths and expectations that so hamper attempts to improve sexual relations.

We then wanted to know what factors facilitate and help to bring about magnificent sex (Chapters 4-12). We defined contributing factors as widely as possible. We were interested in anything that might lead to magnificent sex across time, the qualities of the individuals and their relationships or some combinations. We inquired about everything from the distant past of the individual to recent personal and relational developments, as adult lovers become increasingly intimate (Chapter 4), to whatever partners might do immediately beforehand, in preparation for making sex extraordinary (Chapter 5). (No, it's not about having the bed strewn with rose petals.) We studied the enduring qualities and skills of the individual (Chapter 6) and the relationship (Chapter 9) as compared to the contributors right then and there, *during* sexual activities which helped to make a particular encounter unforgettably erotic and fulfilling (Chapters 7 and 10). That is, whereas most sexual dysfunction/therapy research is concerned with the general factors that lead to sexual difficulties, we were interested in what makes sex magnificent. As such, chapter by chapter we will review the elements in the person, in the relationship both in general and specifically, while engaged in sex which contribute to optimizing erotic experience. We also sought to identify the skills required to make sex extraordinary (Chapter 8). In the course of our research, the roles of heightened empathy and superb communication stood out on multiple levels: as crucial building blocks of optimal sexual experiences; as facilitating factors that helped create anticipation and lead to magnificent sex; as an element that made the experience magnificent *during* sex. Therefore, we devote an entire chapter to empathic communication (Chapter 11). Surprisingly, although the view from the peaks of optimal sexual experiences is remarkably similar, whether from the vantage point of an older, monogamous, heterosexual couple after 50 years of marriage or a 22-year-old bisexual, polyamorous, BDSM aficionado, the paths towards the heights are quite distinctive. We will examine and consider the combinations of contributing factors which create multiple pathways towards more fulfilling sexual relations in Chapter 12.

We continue by discussing the implications and applications of our findings for lovers who want more out of their sex lives, as well as sex and couples therapists who might wish to help clients experience greater heights of erotic intimacy (Chapter 13). That is also where we will circle back to where we began: How can research on extraordinary lovers be of value to couples distressed over low to no sexual frequency/desire (and of course, to their therapists)?

Please note that at every step, we will be emphasizing the plurality of ways of being sexual and of discovering routes towards magnificent sex. It is no secret that the media portray "great sex" as the purview of the young, beautiful and able-bodied, in romantic, monogamous heterosexual relationships. We beg to differ. We have found optimal sexual experiences occur among the young and old, among the healthy as well as disabled or chronically ill and among people with every sexual orientation and proclivity, in monogamous and consensually non-monogamous relationships.

More importantly, this book will be _de_scriptive rather than _pre_scriptive. We will be describing what we have discovered and how our findings _could_ be useful for those who are so inclined. We are not suggesting what anyone _ought_ to do, let alone trying to raise the bar for people's sex lives. For one thing, we promised one of the participants, an older gentleman, that we would honour his wishes (and besides, we agree with him strongly):

> But in terms of how you go about doing it . . . I wouldn't believe a cookbook. If you guys come up with a cookbook and you tell me to follow it, you would have to really convince me that there's a cookbook approach where I can do this . . .
>   P.K.: Relax, we're not planning a cookbook.
> Thank heavens! My wife loves cooking. She follows lots of recipes exactly, often she doesn't. But it turns out great lots of times. Some things can be done without fail. This isn't one of those.

This book is intended for anyone who is interested in learning about truly extraordinary erotic intimacy and how it might be attained. There are too many people diagnosed with sexual desire disorders whose sex lives leave them feeling empty at best or alone and alienated, wondering what all the fuss is about. We are inclined to suggest that their low desire may be evidence of good judgment. We would not expect "normal" people to have strong desires for low quality sex. This book is for them. Their partners, who try and too often feel painfully frustrated and rejected might want to consider the possibility that higher levels of mutual erotic intimacy can be part of the solution to their problems. Or to put it another way, many patients diagnosed with low desire problems will comment, "If I never had sex again, I wouldn't miss it." We have yet to hear an individual who has had magnificent sex express such a sentiment.

Lots of individuals and couples in new relationships or who have been together for a while have a sense that although their sex lives are satisfactory, there might be something more out there. We are here to tell them that their intuitions are correct, to describe what magnificent sex looks like, and for those who wish to put in the time and energy – because it won't just happen spontaneously – what some extraordinary lovers have done to improve their sex lives substantially.

The reader might be a person at midlife or older who is wondering if his or her sexual future is destined to be dismal or non-existent. The reader might be a virgin who is wondering what kinds of sex could be worth the wait. This book is for these people, too.

We are also reaching out to our colleagues in the fields of couples and sex therapy and education. The study of magnificent sex has important educational and clinical applications. Just as too much of what passes for "sex education" is really reproductive biology, too much sex therapy is oriented towards helping clients eliminate sexual dysfunctions so that "normal" sexual functioning can be attained. It is illuminating that after conventional sex therapy alleviates obstacles to sexual intercourse (e.g., erectile dysfunction; MacMahon, Smith & Shabsigh, 2006), patients still seem to maintain their low frequencies of sexual activity. Or they now report new problems, including difficulties with orgasm and low sexual desire. For the sex therapists, this can be conceptualized as symptom substitution, comparable to when a patient triumphantly quits smoking, only to begin eating excessively and gaining 30 lb. More to the point, sometimes the physical symptoms of sexual dysfunctions originate in the body's understandable response to sex that is (or was) mechanically functional but otherwise uninspiring. Our bodies silently plead for sex that makes us feel alive and engaged in one another's embrace; when that is not in reach, our spirits begin to decline, as does the desire for the type of sex that is available.

We are aiming to broaden the field of sexology by adding to our knowledge of the entire spectrum of sexualities, from dysfunctional to "normal" to optimal. We are especially hoping that a clear-eyed, empirically-based look at the farther reaches of human erotic potential can help to inform and expand our methods and goals in working in couples and sex therapy in general and with the most vexing of sexual problems in particular: sexual desire discrepancy. Perhaps a focus on the quality rather than the quantity of sex as perceived by each of the extraordinary lovers can assist clients to find the kinds of erotic intimacy that each could anticipate and savour with delight.

1

HOW DID WE SET OUT TO LEARN ABOUT MAGNIFICENT SEX?

From the Dismal to the Ordinary to Optimal Sexual Experience

R eaders who want to get straight to the good stuff, that is, the ingredients or components of magnificent sex, please feel free to skip ahead to Chapter 2.

In the Western world, "great sex" is the subject of great contradiction in the public sphere. On the one hand, the pursuit of "amazing" sex is represented in media sources as one of the primary goals of humankind. It is assumed to be virtually universal (Rye & Meaney, 2007) based on the covers of women's and men's magazines, the topics discussed on television talk shows, the titles of thousands of self-help books, the proliferation of advice on the Internet and depictions in pornography. It seems clear that great sex is considered very desirable and that many people want to have it (or have more of it) but do not know how to go about this.

Media advice is often characterized by a focus on performance (Duran & Prusank, 1997; Ménard & Kleinplatz, 2008) with suggestions for how to achieve great sex revolving around the use of specific stimulation techniques, new positions and the addition of "novelty" (e.g., using props). Most of the time, media definitions of sexuality (whether optimal or not) tend to be riddled with gender stereotypes and sexual myths. The belief in these myths may actually engender sexual problems rather than fixing them.

Despite the evident interest from the general public, the vast majority of the literature on sexual functioning is focused on sexual dysfunction, with thousands of studies on erectile dysfunction, premature ejaculation, low desire, sexual arousal disorder and other kinds of difficulties and problems. Normal sexual functioning, which has received much less research attention, is often equated with normal physiological functioning. However, many individuals who have impaired physiological functioning (i.e., who are unable to engage in intercourse or orgasm) are not distressed by this (Ferenidou et al., 2008; King, Holt & Nazareth, 2007; Shifren et al., 2008) whereas many others, who have "normal" physiological functioning, are nevertheless dissatisfied with the quality of their sexual experiences (Leiblum, 2010; Schnarch, 2000). The inevitable conclusion from the focus on sexual dysfunction is that optimal sexual experiences are by default equated with the absence of sexual dysfunctions.

The lack of attention in the literature to wonderful sexual experiences reflects the overall trend in psychology to focus on the negative aspects of human experience. In general, research or theory about how to bring about wonderful, incredible, optimal or peak experiences of any kind (i.e., sexual or non-sexual) is lacking, with notable exceptions. Humanistic psychologist Abraham Maslow used the term "peak experience" to describe those "moments of highest happiness and fulfillment" (1968, p. 73). He characterized these peak experiences as mystic and ecstatic, involving a sense of great awe, intense happiness or bliss (1962). Mahrer studied optimal behaviours, which included welcoming the moment; being attuned, receptive and responsive to bodily-felt sensations; being open and welcoming to different parts of the self; and appreciating the personal world of others (2008, 2009). Similarly, some sex therapists have suggested that wonderful sex includes such elements as communication, a focus on pleasure rather than performance, a non-genital focus, openness, variety, intimacy, relaxation, anticipation, affection, orgasm and ecstasy (Barbach, 2000; Broder & Goldman, 2004; Castleman, 2004; Kleinplatz, 1996b, 2006; Metz & McCarthy, 2010, 2012; Morin, 1995; Ogden, 1999, 2006; Resnick, 1997, 2012; Schnarch, 1991, 2009; Shaw, 2012). This clinical work provides an alternative to media definitions of "great sex".

Because the academic study of sexuality has focused primarily on dysfunctional or normal sexuality, the topic of optimal sexual experiences has been marginalized and neglected. The result is that our understanding of sexual experiences is incomplete at best. That left us plenty of room to begin studying magnificent sex.

What Questions Were We Trying to Answer?

The first thing we needed to learn was what makes some sex magnificent. That has two meanings: How would one describe the elements that comprise optimal sexual experience? That is, what is it about these experiences that is unique or distinctive? How are they different from everyday sex or from good or even very good sex? How would you recognize "great" sex if you stumbled into it? The second meaning of our opening question is: What leads to or can account for the occurrence of extraordinary sex? What factors facilitate the experience of extraordinary erotic intimacy? These were our opening queries. We needed to answer the first set of questions before we could later identify how to bring about magnificent sex.

Our goal for the first study in this project was to identify and understand the components that constitute optimal sexual experience. This was a crucial stage for several reasons. When we embarked on this research, there were no empirical definitions of "great sex" or "optimal sexual experiences" or "wonderful sex" or "fantastic sex" or any conceptually-related ideas available in the academic or sex therapy research literature. We needed to define our terms to ensure that it was clear what was meant by magnificent sex and that participants' responses were comparable, that is, that they were talking about the same kind of experience.

This research was conducted within the framework of "descriptive phenomenology", an approach to gathering data that is used within discovery-oriented, qualitative methodologies to produce descriptions of previously-unexplored phenomena. Phenomenological researchers aim to grasp the richness of a phenomenon from different participants' subjective realities / experiences.

But which participants would be required? In phenomenological research models, one seeks out individuals who have particular knowledge and experience in the area under investigation (known as "key informants"). It seemed that the most obvious and accurate way to answer our questions was to consult with individuals and couples who had developed expertise in this area, that is, people who had experienced magnificent sex.

Who Did We Decide to Talk to and Why?

My [P.J.K.] clinical experience had given me a glimpse as to who might be the sought-after experts: Most of us are raised to think of sex through a fairly narrow lens. The circumscribed definition of "sex" often becomes one of the obstacles to enjoying sex fully. I had noticed that among my clients, many of those who had found unique avenues for the fullness of sexual expression had been those who had gone beyond the parameters of conventional definitions of sex. Some of these seemed on the outside to be quite ordinary individuals. They worked hard, raised children and had been married for many years. Why were they in my office? Sometimes they came to sex therapy because life had handed them a new challenge: One of them had developed cancer or heart disease or diabetes. A family member had died. There had been a job loss or a retirement. A new medication had affected sexual functioning. An astute primary care physician had noticed that a change in their lives after many years of marriage was beginning to disrupt their sexual relationship and had referred them to me. It struck me as ironic and meaningful that precisely the matters that had challenged them now created new opportunities for growth and development. It was like the old curse, "May you live in interesting times." These couples were typically older and were ready to face whatever lay ahead by deepening their levels of intimacy. Here, when I refer to intimacy, this is not a euphemism for sex. Rather, the quality of their sexuality and emotional intimacy seemed to provide the foundations for erotic development in the face of tough times. How illuminating that these seemingly ordinary, older couples – the ones we typically think of as the marketing targets for KY-jelly and Viagra – revealed how extraordinary they could become as lovers once life forced them to redefine sexual intimacy.

Similarly, some of the others who had, of necessity, learned to think outside the box in order to redefine themselves as sexual beings were members of sexual/gender minority groups. These might be individuals who were lesbian, gay, bisexual, trans, queer or questioning (LGBTQ) or who might identify as into BDSM (i.e., bondage and discipline or dominance and submission or sexual sadomasochism or some combination) or kink. They might be individuals in consensually non-monogamous relationships. In therapy, I had noticed that anyone who had had to re-envision sexuality en route to full sexual expression stood a pretty good chance of ultimately having an out-of-this-world sex life.

These were my clinical impressions. It was now time for a broader, empirical study of magnificent sex. These insights, however, proved a useful starting place for our team to think about who to recruit for our research. Who, we wondered, would have this experience or expertise? For the reasons enumerated above and below, participants recruited for this study consisted of (1) individuals over the age of 60 who had been in a relationship for 25 years or more, (2) self-identified members of sexual minority groups and (3) sex therapists.

The sexuality of older people has often been marginalized in mainstream media representations. In magazines, romance novels, television shows and movies, "great" sexual experiences are usually reserved for young, attractive, able-bodied individuals. It is assumed that older people are post-sexual, or that if they are sexual, they suffer from multiple dysfunctions and require help from pharmaceuticals. However, existing research and theories on non-sexual peak or optimal experiences have shown that these kinds of experiences may be more likely for older individuals. In the last few years, the results from several large-scale studies have shown that older individuals can and do enjoy sex into their 60s, 70s, 80s and beyond (e.g., Traeen, Štulhofer, Jurin & Hald, 2018). We thought that there might be much to learn from those who continued to pursue optimal sexual experiences well into old age. Older individuals who have managed to make a relationship last for 25 years or more might possess valuable knowledge about what makes for lasting and fulfilling sexual relations. In fact, a few authors have suggested that sexual satisfaction improves with the age and length of the relationship (e.g., Schnarch, 1991; Shaw, 2012; Zilbergeld, 2004). To this end, we interviewed 30 older men and women, ranging in age from 60 to 82 years (with an average age of 65.8 years old).

Similarly to older individuals, the behaviours and beliefs of individuals who identify as lesbian, gay, bisexual, transgender, queer, polyamorous and/or kinky have been deemed pathological by some health professionals. Group members have often been marginalized within society, poorly treated by social institutions and denied basic rights. However, an important factor in bringing about magnificent sex might be an individual's willingness to experiment, to take risks and to question conventional thinking. Due to their sexual orientations or preferences, it seems likely that many sexual minority group members may have been forced to re-evaluate the relevance of normative sexual scripts for them. There may be much to learn from those who have had the courage to step outside the prevailing cultural sexual scripts. Indeed, writings produced by self-identified BDSM practitioners (e.g., Califia, 1994; Ortmann & Sprott, 2013; Shahbaz & Chirinos, 2017; Sprott & Hadcock, 2017) suggest that their activities played a part in bringing about optimal sexual experiences. These writers emphasize the need for deep levels of trust and communication in their practice of BDSM, qualities that might be very relevant to optimal sexual experiences. We interviewed 13 men, 11 women and one self-identified "genderqueer" individual, ranging in age from 22 to 59 years, with an average age of 45.2 years old.

In the case of both the older participants and the sexual minority group members, we had been worried about whether or not we would find enough participants for our research. Much to our surprise, our initial queries snowballed such that within a few weeks, we had more volunteers than we could possibly interview. Phenomenological research methods call for depth of interviews rather than large sample sizes; a typical phenomenological study might have 8 to 12 or so participants. The important criterion is to interview enough participants so as to gather a well-rounded and comprehensive picture of the phenomenon in question. We had an embarrassment of riches and interviewed more participants (a total of 75) than is common in other phenomenological studies to date in the literature. Nothing like this had been done before, but as it turned out, these choices were rather apt. We had a great deal to learn from the people we came to call "extraordinary lovers".

In addition, we added one more group of participants, that is, sex therapists. Although there was not much information in the academic literature on optimal sexual experiences, the little that we could find had been produced by clinicians who practise sex therapy. We anticipated that sex therapists might have spent considerable time reflecting on the subject of the quality of sexual experiences in order to assist their clients in developing treatment goals. In total, 20 sex therapists were interviewed, a group consisting of 11 men and nine women. These participants were recruited from a listserv for sex therapy and research professionals.

Unlike the other participants, sex therapists were not asked to provide additional demographic information (e.g., age, marital status) as we were not anticipating that they would be speaking about their own personal experiences of magnificent sex (although some chose to do so).

How Did We Go about Collecting Data?

Procedure

Participants were recruited in a variety of ways. Older individuals in long-term relationships were recruited from associations, social groups and community groups from advertisements placed on bulletin boards and online. Individuals from sexual minority groups (i.e., BDSM, LGBTQ, poly) were recruited from a post on a listserv for self-identified kink/BDSM practitioners. In the recruitment blurbs, we sought out individuals who self-identified as having "great", "remarkable", "wonderful" and "memorable" sex. (We used colloquial language rather than "optimal sexual experience" because the term had yet to be defined empirically.) In addition, sex therapists were recruited from a post on a listserv for sex therapists because we had hoped that they might have insights on the entire spectrum of sexual experiences.

Participant interviews were conducted over the telephone by both authors because this allowed us to reach a wider group of people and this procedure increased participants' comfort levels by ensuring a high degree of anonymity. We interviewed individuals from all over Canada and the United States, as well as a few from Europe and the Middle East.

We generated a set of interview questions and then reviewed them with three sexologists prior to the commencement of interviews. For example, questions included, "What is great sex?", "What leads to great sex?" and "How would you recognize great sex if you stumbled into it?" The interviews lasted between 42 minutes and 110 minutes, with an average length of 80 minutes. The average transcript length was 31 double-spaced pages.

In phenomenological research, the emphasis in every phase of the research process is to stay as close as possible to "the thing itself" (Polkinghorne, 1989, 1994). As such, we will be presenting our findings by using extensive quotes from the participants in our study, that is, the words of extraordinary lovers.

The research team

At the outset of the research project, a team of volunteers was assembled to assist us in data analysis. Since the beginning of the project in the fall of 2005, the composition of the team has varied but has included clinical psychologists, physicians, counsellors, psychotherapists, educators and students in human kinetics, nursing, medicine and psychology. Apart from the original interviewers [P.J.K. and A.D.M.], the interviews were masked. That is, the rest of the research team members were kept "blind" to the demographic information of the participants, meaning that they were not told the age or sex of the interviewee or what type of participants they were (i.e., male, female, kinky, older).

Within the team, efforts were made to set aside our personal thoughts, biases, assumptions, presuppositions, judgments and beliefs about wonderful sex in order to bring a fresh perspective to the research. This process required a lot of rigorous self-reflection and was often a topic of discussion during team meetings.

Data analysis

To identify the components and contributing factors of magnificent sex, a subset of interview transcripts were provided to team members and they were asked to read each of them in their entirety. When a preliminary organization system was agreed upon, we tested our understanding of the components by labelling a selection of participant statements using the developing coding system with new transcripts. This test was followed by a return to the transcripts and refinement of the categorization system. Finally, over the course of two years of careful analysis, we were able to identify eight major components and over the following five years, the seven contributing factors with sufficient accuracy and consistency. The percentage of agreement among seven raters and across 75 transcripts ranged from 70% to 93% over the course of the research.

Serendipity: Group differences and similarities

As part of the larger research endeavour, it was immediately apparent that the rest of the research team members, that is, those who were not present during the phone interviews but only received carefully de-identified transcripts, could not distinguish male from female participants, old from young, "kinky" from "vanilla", and disabled from able-bodied participants. Given the focus on gender differences and other group distinctions in mainstream conceptualizations, we were struck by this unexpected finding. By contrast, despite the masked transcripts, our research team colleagues easily and accurately detected the sex therapists, whose ideas often diverged markedly from participants who had actually experienced magnificent sex. We will return to these distinctions at the end of Chapter 3.

PART II

PART II

2

THE COMPONENTS
OF MAGNIFICENT SEX

What Do We Mean by Components? How Did We Know People Were Talking about the Same Phenomenon?

What do we mean by components? How are we defining the components of optimal sexual experience? Here we are talking about the constituent parts, the atoms that make up magnificent sex, the fundamental ingredients, the *sine qua non* of the experience. Lay people's reactions to the question "What is great sex?" were often something along these lines: "Oh, I know. It's orgasm for men, relationship for women." That was not what we found at all. One of the first surprising findings was the universality of the components across different groups – men and women, young and old, LGBTQ and straight, monogamous and consensually non-monogamous, kinky and "vanilla" (that is, non-kinky). The uncanny similarity in descriptions helped us to become reasonably certain that everyone *was* talking about the same experience. In essence, the components of magnificent sex represent the view from the top of a mountain. (In Chapter 12, it will become clear that although the view from the peak may be the same, people take different routes to reach the top.)

In addition, we went out of our way to ask open-ended questions so that the people we interviewed could define their optimal experiences in their own ways. For example, we would ask about good sex, very good sex, great sex and the three best sexual experiences of their lives. By the time participants had finished differentiating among these different categories in their own minds and in our interviews, it was pretty clear that they were referring to the same phenomenon when they got to "great" or "best". Some people were waiting for us to define terms for them and said so at the outset of the interview. We replied that we truly had no answers; we explained that this was not hypothesis-testing but rather discovery-oriented research. We sought out these experts in order to teach us – and we told them so. Thus, as the questions progressed, it became increasingly obvious that we had designed the prompts in order to have the participants define terms for us, thereby creating empirically-based definitions that would guide us in future research and clinical applications.

Please note: We are certainly not trying to say that the eight components we discovered represent how everyone defines or experiences magnificent sex. On the contrary, these are the results we found from talking to particular groups of people, at particular times in their lives. Our intention is not to set these findings into stone or codify them into law.

The Eight Major Components of Magnificent Sex

1. Being Completely Present in the Moment, Embodied, Focused, Absorbed

The first major ingredient or component of magnificent sex is the feeling of being completely present, immersed and absorbed in the moment as it unfolds. This feeling of being utterly engrossed was frequently cited as the major difference between great sex and merely average or even very good sex. It stood out as the first and most prominent element emphasized by almost everyone. One man we interviewed expressed disappointment that such a simple concept could be so important: "Now I'm just talking about that stupid 'being present' stuff . . . unfortunately, that's the truth. It really is about being present." Interestingly enough, friends, family and acquaintances who asked about the research often spontaneously volunteered that their best sexual experiences were those in which they felt completely absorbed. It's interesting that there could be high levels of consensus across such diverse groups on a phenomenon that is seemingly so complicated. At the end of the day, what many of us are looking for is to feel that we are all there, alive in one another's embrace.

Being present during magnificent sex means being focused on all levels – mentally, physically, emotionally and spiritually. People talked about being aware of the sensations experienced moment to moment and feeling completely embodied. This means slowing down and being fully conscious, "inside the moment". As one participant described it, "You're not a person in a situation. You *are* it. You *are* the situation." One man described being present as, "Feeling my body, being aware that my body was there, and liking it." A few people compared this sense of immersion in the experience with Csíkszentmihályi's description of "flow", that is, "the state in which people are so involved in an activity that nothing else seems to matter; the experience itself is so enjoyable that people will do it even at great cost, for the sheer sake of doing it" (1990, p. 4). (Ironically, Csíkszentmihályi has stated on several occasions that he did not believe that sexual activities are likely to lead to flow states. No doubt, extraordinary lovers would disagree strongly.)

Some said that magnificent sex can be recognized as such only after the fact because the act of noticing and labelling the experience as magnificent would automatically remove one's attention from the moment itself. As one woman explained, "When it's happening, you're not thinking about anything else except what is happening." Most people said that dealing with internal and external distractions was a major challenge to being present; many reported that learning the skills to cope with distractions was an important contributor to developing the capacity for optimal sexual experiences. Participants told us that being entirely absorbed and embodied during optimal sexual experiences left no room for worrying about household chores, work, finances, children, etc. One woman explained how mental distractions could help determine whether she was having mediocre versus magnificent sex:

> The difference is when I can really just let go and completely focus and be in the moment and not have that, you know, running commentary going through my head about anything else. Either running commentary about, you know, 'Ooh, is the lighting right, do I look good, you know, should I, you know, move my hand over here?' all the way to the running commentary of, 'Ooh, it's Monday night, um, I need to remember to take the trash out when we're done'. That, um, that, that's a sign that I'm having a mediocre sex experience [laughing]. A great sex experience for me is when that little soundtrack in my head completely goes away and it's not a matter of should I move my hand here, my hand just goes there because that's where it's supposed to go, that's where it's. And, you know, I don't think about anything except what is happening each second and what I'm feeling, and the energy being exchanged between me and my partner and the, the – how, how they're reacting, how I'm reacting. Everything else, you know, the, the room can be on fire and I probably wouldn't even notice.

There is a beautiful simplicity to this description. So many magazines and books have been sold on the promise of helping people have "great sex" and they are full of bows, frills, whistles and acrobatics. Actually, these things may be more likely to distract if they take lovers out of the moment. Optimal sexual experiences are simultaneously much simpler and also more complicated than this.

In the ten years or so since we first published our data on being present (Kleinplatz & Ménard, 2007), much of it has been misconstrued as "mindfulness". Mindfulness, as described by ancient Buddhists and Hindus, was part of a lifelong discipline with the goal of spiritual enlightenment. Training in brief, mindfulness-based interventions has been part of a revolution in psychotherapy and even in sex therapy (Brotto, 2018), which we applaud. In fact, mindfulness and being present as described by our participants are qualitatively, different states of being (to be discussed further in Chapter 8). Furthermore, it is one thing to be centered while alone in a room, practising "mindfulness", and quite another to be embodied within *while* being connected during sex with one's partner. That is more of a challenge and brings us to our next component.

2. Connection, Alignment, Being in Synch, Merger

If the first component is about one's own state, the second is about the self in relation with another (or others). Please note that the tricky part we will need to return to later is being capable of being fully present and embodied within, while being fully engaged with and in synch with another.

Feeling absolutely connected with one's sexual partner is the second major component of magnificent sex. One woman defined this as, "At least one moment, the snap of the fingers, the length of a heartbeat, a breath where I can't tell where I stop and they start." Others used words like "alignment" or "synchronicity" or "merger." Another woman compared connecting with a sexual partner to "bridging a gap." Some people used words borrowed from physics, as in "electricity", "energy" and "conductivity". One woman described connection as:

> The energy between people that wraps itself around them like a blanket to the point where you notice the creation of the body between them more than you notice either one of the individuals involved.

"I just feel like our, our cells and molecules are just merging", said one man. One person described this feeling as, "There's a light, people who are having great sex, you get the feeling that even if they're in the dark, they glow in the dark." Others used metaphors and analogies drawn from the world of religion and art.

> You just are completely in the flow and yeah, you know intellectually
> that you're separate people, but everything in your immediate expe-
> rience is as if you're completely . . . all of the outlines have dissolved
> and it's like the Klimt painting, where you really can't tell where the
> bodies are, that they just all merge and all you feel is the flow.

It seems as though we continue to struggle with a paucity of words for cap-
turing the essence of sexual experiences. Is it any wonder that many people
struggle with enhancing sexuality when we have not had a good roadmap and
sometimes lack an adequate vocabulary to describe where we would like to go?

As part of the interview, we asked almost everyone how they would recognize
great sex if they "stumbled" into it. Some people talked about unexpectedly finding themselves having an optimal sexual experience. Others would ask, "What
do you mean, *stumbled* into it?" Still others had attended sex parties (private or
public) and could talk about this idea on a more literal level. As in, "Do you mean,
if I were at a party with dozens of people having sex, how would I recognize the
ones having the greatest sex if I stumbled across them?" As always, we encouraged them to answer questions in their own ways, so we responded, "Yes, sure."
One such woman highlighted the importance of connection in her answer:

> I would see them laughing perhaps, or um, so intensely engaged
> with each other that there's no room for, um, outside, um, inter-
> ference with that. I mean, in other words, they're not even notic-
> ing the rest of world. And that they would be uninhibited and
> enthralled with each other.

Another woman talked about this idea of connection by describing her
experience of watching pornography:

> . . . if they were giving oral sex to them they would look like that
> was the, there was nothing else they'd rather be doing right at that
> moment. That's, that's when I think I, if I stumbled on that I'd say,
> 'Oh my God. These two people are really having a good time with
> each other.' That's, that's how I would know. If I could see the
> man's expression, and he looked like he was lost in what he was
> doing and he was loving it and the two of them were, you know,
> looking, their facial expressions were, it could be that agony look
> of ecstasy, but I could tell.

Many reported that being present and feeling connected are pieces of optimal sexual experiences that are almost invariably intertwined. Several talked

about "being present *in* the connection". This makes intuitive sense: How can one be connected to another if one is not truly present? Part of what makes this connection so remarkable for many is the simultaneous letting go. Some people described this sensation as feeling like one person as opposed to two or not feeling separate from the other. One woman said, "At that moment, there was no one else in my world. That person became the center of my universe for that exchange. That relationship was all there was in my awareness." Some compared this feeling of connection to living in a shared, common experience. As one man said, "Inside my body I'm the other person's body and we're just kind of all one together at that moment." When we asked another man to define great sex, his answer was, "The first element is just getting lost in one another, consumed, lost." Another man described connection as, "A melding, blurring of identity boundaries so that one feels like you were literally feeling with the other and the distinction between what the other person feels and what you feel seem almost irrelevant." In many ways, this seems to tap into some of our deepest longings as human beings. We long to lose ourselves in something bigger. As one man said, we want to "quiet the existential angst".

It also stands in contrast to at least some of the couples therapy literature which emphasizes the need for separateness in order to come together (Perel, 2006; Schnarch, 2009). Although this literature focuses on differentiation and warns against fusion or merger as preventing enduring intimacy, our extraordinary lovers would have us question this notion. It is not couples and sex therapists who describe this phenomenon but poets and songwriters who speak of two hearts that beat as one (see Kleinplatz, Ménard, Paquet et al., 2009).

On the other hand, what may be required is a blend of separateness with erotic union, with different emphases across different individuals and relationships.

3. Deep Sexual and Erotic Intimacy

Although feelings of connection and merger could be experienced in a relationship of any duration, for some people, magnificent sex cannot be separated from the relationship in which it happens. In response to our first question of the interview, one man said: "What is great sex? You know, if I were going to answer glibly, it'd be great relationship." For many, the intensity and depth of the intimacy they shared with their partners was a major component of what made sex magnificent. One woman, who reported having had a lot of casual sex, said: "I don't know that I'm capable of having great sex anymore without really caring about a partner. It would just be flat." The identification of this component of optimal sexual experiences was not a big surprise. However, many of our colleagues and the laypeople with whom we discussed this research assumed that this component would be the exclusive emphasis of women. Instead, we heard about the importance of deep intimacy from almost everyone we interviewed. Some people had had magnificent sex with many partners; others had had magnificent sex with only a few (and sometimes just one partner). Some expressed doubt that they would ever be able to have extraordinary sex with anyone but their long-term partners.

This component of magnificent sex is characterized by deep feelings of mutual respect and trust for their partners. As one woman put it, "That was my instinct with both of my partners when I first met them: I always tell people it wasn't love at first sight, it was trust at first sight." People talked about caring, valuing and liking their partners; interestingly, very, very few of those we interviewed identified love as a characteristic of intimacy. In fact, many defined virtually every facet of love without using that particular word. Is love too simple a term or is it too complicated? Extraordinary lovers certainly demonstrated linguistic precision; maybe they wanted to be crystal clear in what they meant with regard to their own feelings. Or perhaps love is the potential result of this kind of intimacy – following from trust, respect, caring, etc. However, the love that people felt for their partners was implicit in their words. This was especially true when both members of a couple were interviewed separately.

4. Extraordinary Communication and Deep Empathy

Extraordinary communication was a recurring theme across interviews. In this chapter, we are specifically referring to communication per se as a *component* of magnificent sex, that is, a part of what makes it great. However, communication between partners is also a major *contributor*, helping to bring magnificent sex about and make it possible.

Extraordinary lovers told us about the joys of verbal and non-verbal communication before, during and after sex. Many reported that being able to share themselves completely with another person was a major part of what made sex extraordinary. As one woman described it, "Freeing and very liberating." People told us that getting the opportunity to reveal parts of themselves that are not usually shared was exhilarating, and taking verbal risks with their partners was a wonderful way to push back their own limits. Others described the joy of receiving such communications from a partner. They talked about the importance of verbal communication as well as "hands-on" demonstrations. As one woman put it:

> It can also be grabbing your partner's hand and placing your hand over it and helping them figure out what it is that works for you. Not everyone can communicate verbally outside of the bed, or kitchen counter or coffee table.

Some defined communication itself as a sexual act; others stated that certain sex acts constituted a way to communicate. One man described an extraordinary sexual encounter consisting entirely of communication and erotic awareness, where neither partner touched the other physically. (Being on the receiving end of stories such as this unique, memorable encounter was part of the magic of conducting this research. It was a privilege for us to listen to people who had the courage to share so openly and vividly with us.) Others defined certain sex acts (e.g., kissing, intercourse) as a form of communication with their partners.

The importance of kissing came up several times, which is noteworthy because we often forget about kissing and how crucial it can be in long-term relationships. In the movies, kissing signals beginnings, rather than enduring eroticism. A sex therapist stated:

> If one thinks of sexual intercourse as the apex of all intercourse, of social intercourse that sexual relationship becomes the epitome of the best kind of communication we have between partners.

Certainly, this suggests the need to redefine and refine what we mean when we say that something constitutes a "sex act".

The importance of communication for magnificent sex is hardly surprising. However, the way it was defined and explained by extraordinary lovers is quite different from the way people talk about sexual communication in other arenas (e.g., sex and couples therapists, media). This isn't "a little to the left" territory, it is all-consuming. If you want to make sex extraordinary, you are almost signing up to be consumed – both in the act, and in working towards it. Contrast the apparent pervasiveness of sex, the idea that "everyone's talking about sex, it's everywhere", with the actual shallowness of these discussions. In essence, we're talking about it but not well.

The research suggests that even – or perhaps especially – among their peers, even the ostensibly, sexually open, emerging adults deliberately communicate in the vaguest terms, such as "make out" or "hook up" so as to obscure what they actually mean out of fear of their friends' judgments (Plante, 2006).

Talking about sex openly so as to be understood fully is difficult and takes courage. Our fellow couples therapists aren't helping. In the professional literature, there is a great deal of attention to the role of effective communication skills in maintaining relationships. Therapists focus on teaching couples how to validate, paraphrase, make "I" statements, particularly during conflict. But effective communication will merely get couples to efficient and functional sex. By contrast, the people we interviewed were black-belt communicators, willing to share their bodies and souls nakedly, unmistakably and divulging all. Their communication was alive, engaging, compelling, vivid and inviting. And from what we could infer, they excelled not only in verbal communication but also in active and receptive touch. Many lovers touch with curiosity and eagerness to explore in the early phases of their sexual relationships. Later on, however, their touch becomes rote, intended to literally go through the motions that will lead to expedient satisfaction rather than the heights of erotic discovery. It was clear that extraordinary lovers continually renew their knowledge of their partners via their bodies; they touch so as to really feel and allow themselves to be felt through their skin. These individuals are able to be fully present in their own skin while simultaneously able to let go enough to embody the other's space.

5. Being Genuine, Authentic, Transparent

Having the opportunity to be completely, genuinely and honestly themselves is, for many, the hallmark of a magnificent sexual experience. People described the freedom to be uninhibited and unselfconscious, sharing their private desires, interests or fantasies within a context of complete trust and acceptance. One woman defined authenticity as, "The ability to share . . . realness of yourself . . . real feelings, really what's going on." A man thought that magnificent sex involved, "Being able to be selfish, impulsive, free of cares, unguarded, unplanned, in the moment, emotionally available, emotionally uncontrolled." We often find the opportunity to explore ways of being during magnificent sex that are not afforded to us outside of it. Many of us don't inhabit worlds where we are encouraged to let go fully. We don't live a culture that privileges or promotes authenticity, with certain notable exceptions (e.g., Brené Brown).

Extraordinary lovers described feeling completely uninhibited during magnificent sex, giving themselves permission to revel in pleasure and enjoy the experience as fully as possible. One man said that magnificent sex involved the opportunity to "reveal parts of yourself in a very different way" and "dealing with some essential truth about yourself." As another person commented, "It's the thing that makes me feel the freest."

Many described the pleasure of being totally transparent and available with a lover; they also talked about the joy at receiving such revelations from their partners. As one man said, ". . . a person telling me something very, very private about themselves – that would turn me on." One woman described her reaction during a revealing sexual encounter with her husband, "It was just so shocking to me that I could actually express these things and, he was right there loving it and doing it with me." Another woman described the pleasure she took in her partners' reactions to her offerings:

> Getting to that point where I am completely stripped bare emo-
> tionally, physically, you know, spiritually. If they can reach in, and
> grab whatever they want, and take it out, look at it, play with it,
> you know, whatever and I love it.

For many, the experience of magnificent sex also represented an opportunity to develop, pursue, explore and expand on their own capacities for authenticity and genuineness. "You're acting on instinct and that's when you really know who you are," said one woman. Another described magnificent sex as, "an opportunity to connect or deal with some essential truth about yourself." One man defined great sex as sex where "you found your voice." Getting comfortable with being uncomfortable may be an important skill for developing the capacity for magnificent sex.

6. Vulnerability and Surrender

It is one thing to be genuine and authentic alone; it is hard enough to look oneself in the mirror honestly when there are no witnesses. However, this next component involves a step beyond that: It entails choosing to be emotionally naked while in full view of another.

Many people said that being able to be vulnerable and surrender, both to the sex itself and to their partners, is a crucial component of magnificent sex. "Letting go", being "swept away" or "taken" and "going with the flow" were phrases that often came up in connection with this idea. One man described it as, "A sense of really almost not being there anymore and just sort of being fucking. And a sense of . . . being swept away in the act." A woman asked, "If you're not going to give yourself up to it, then what's the point?" An older man described his experience of surrendering in the context of magnificent sex:

> Uh, in normal good sex or good relationships, I think there's always some, um, maybe small but detectable barriers, um, some things held back. In great sex, I think those for me disappear and so that one is, uh, uh, quite transparent to the other person and therefore quite, uh, vulnerable but it feels, it goes with an intensely erotic and a good feeling rather than a scary feeling.

One man described his greatest sex as, "absolute loss in my lover's body and, and our activities, to the point where it's otherworldly, out-of-body experience."

Several people independently compared the act of being vulnerable and surrendering during optimal sexual experiences with jumping off a cliff:

> Sex is a leap of faith . . . It's saying I'm going to jump off this cliff where I'm going to, you know, be naked and be vulnerable and give myself, um, to somebody else and take them in and, uh, yeah I hope I feel good after I do that.

Quite a few cited a loss of conscious thought during magnificent sex. One woman explained, "It's not a matter of should I move my hand here, my hand just goes there because that's where it's supposed to go." Reverting to pure, pre-conscious desires was a recurring theme. An older man said, "It's not like you have to do something, it's like you just have to *not* do things, let it . . . You can't push a river but you can sure let it flow." Another man described his experience of surrendering control, "I'm directing my body and moving [laughs], and then all of a sudden, my body is just moving and I have no clue where that's coming from." An older woman stated:

> I think in order for it to be great, it would have to, um, include losing myself enough to be able to reach that height of excitement and then to release it. So kind of that unconscious place, you know, where you just give it up during the orgasm, you know, that inevitability place where you're no longer thinking.

The notions of deliberately letting go, surrendering and being vulnerable are not especially popular in our culture.

7. Exploration, Interpersonal Risk-Taking and Fun

Many said that magnificent sex often involves taking risks and exploring. In this context, the word "risk" is not defined in terms of conventional sexual risk-taking, that is, STIs, pregnancy, sexual violence, etc. Rather, risk-taking in extraordinary sex means encounters where lovers can play, push or expand their own personal boundaries. As one man explained, "There was a sense of danger, in a way, but not the kind of danger where you felt a threat, just a sense of going beyond yourself." He talked about finding "surprising moments of newness" with his wife of 40+ years. Extraordinary lovers describe magnificent sex as an opportunity to go exploring or adventuring, setting out on a journey with a trusted partner. Exploration and risk-taking during sex can provide an opportunity for "discovering stuff about your partner but discovering things about yourself," as one man put it. A woman asked:

> Where can we take each other, where can we go? What private haven of pleasure and connection can we discover for ourselves? What hidden alcove, what ferny grotto? I want to go to those places . . . I certainly haven't done the entire map, as it were.

A sense of play, fun, humour and lightness are important parts of taking risks. Magnificent sex is a way to relax, experiment and not worry about making mistakes. One woman described her favorite sexual partners as those who could, "be silly and can play, you know, like kids . . . explore it." Another woman said, "We're playing with each other, it's just not a sandbox with Tonka toys anymore." One woman explained why she thought optimal sexual experiences involve an element of fun:

> When people actually get right down to it, *it looks funny as hell!* We're making these weird little noises that don't usually come up in casual conversation, and we're in these contorted, awkward positions grunting like animals, folding ourselves up into a sexual origami that hardly resembles anything as elegant as a crane [laughing]. And we're rolling around and we're swapping bodily fluids and we're making big messes and sex is *goofy!* It's absolutely one of the most hilarious things that human beings are capable of. You've got to have a sense of humour.

Several talked about the importance of laughter during optimal sexual experience. One man mentioned, "I always laugh a little bit, at some point either at the beginning, at the end or in the middle." A woman put it simply: "If you're not having fun, it's not great." (Laughter and jokes during interviews were another unexpected bonus of conducting this research. It never felt like work to do these interviews.)

These are important ideas and they do not get the attention they deserve in mainstream culture. People often worry about the right techniques, the best positions and sexual performance. Instead of concerns about getting it right, how often do we talk about the idea of playing, of having unadulterated fun, of making mistakes during sex and recovering from them? Sexual relations can serve as a way to let go, an outlet for tensions and an oasis for pure, sensual delight in the face of everyday stressors.

More importantly, how many of us continue to explore ourselves, let alone via sexuality? Do we keep pushing our own limits sexually? Although we often see recommendations in the media to try new lingerie, new positions and new toys, how often do these recommendations suggest real exploration of self? The possibility of using sex as an avenue for personal development and interpersonal growth was one of the special appeals of sex to extraordinary lovers. This is a crucial aspect of what makes the best sex erotic. A partner can facilitate the process of uncovering and discovery. We will return to the theme of lovers as potential catalysts in the course of sexual explorations in Chapter 13.

8. Transcendence and Transformation

For many, magnificent sex tends to involve experiences of transcendence. As one man said in an exasperated tone, "It's an experience of sort of transcendent, you know, and I'm almost rolling my eyes because I didn't want to use any words like that . . ." Several of the participants had begun the interviews by asking, "So what is it you want to hear us say, here? Are you looking for the 'down and dirty' or the 'touchy-feely'?" And we would have to explain that this was discovery-oriented research rather than hypothesis-testing methodology; it was up to them to tell us about their experiences in their own ways. And so some responded, "Well get ready because I'm about to tell you about the unfiltered, down and dirty parts of hot sex!" It was thus ironic that an hour later, they were describing magnificent sex in exalted, even sacred terms. Having people say during interviews that magnificent sex is transcendent was not especially surprising; however, the sheer number who did, including those who did not identify as religious or spiritual, was unanticipated.

Magnificent sex is described as a combination of heightened states – mental, emotional, physical, relational and spiritual. One woman said, "Great sex is . . . transcendental sex. It goes beyond the physical to a much higher plane of dissolution and merger." Some used terms such as "blissful", "peaceful", "soulful", "ecstatic", "other-worldly" and "out-of-body" or made reference to their souls. One man described an optimal sexual encounter as, "An experience of floating in the universe of light and stars and music and sublime peace." Others used language related to time such as "timeless" or "sense of the infinite". One man explained, "Being transported somewhere else or transcending something where great sex is, like time just disappears." Another man said:

> It really transported me . . . sort of out of time and space and into some delirium of ecstasy that I found really life-affirming and exciting. It was as if the common-place stuff just disappeared and then the intensity of the interaction really sort of blossomed into an all-encompassing feeling of ecstasy and creativity.

As one man said, "The truly great ones really take me and the person I'm with . . . to another realm. And it really takes me almost out of my body even as I'm very much in it." This component may provide another explanation as to why the focus on the physical aspects of sex in *Cosmo* is so misplaced. The data consistently converge showing that the physical is fairly irrelevant to magnificent sex.

A few individuals used language borrowed from religion, e.g., magnificent sex as, "a gift from God", even if they did not personally identify as religious believers, thereby illuminating, again, the paucity of our language for describing optimal erotic experiences. One man said that he and his partner had had a "white lightning experience . . . that was probably only a couple of seconds . . . but it felt eternal." He went on to say, "At this moment, we were in the presence of God." Another man said that one of the things he loved most about sex was, "It takes me away from the mundane." This component provides another illustration of the limitations of language as they relate to optimal sexual experience. Magnificent sex can be other-worldly. Extraordinary sexual experiences are an opportunity to be ourselves in ways that we don't usually have access to (such as being fully present, utterly authentic).

Many expressed the belief that magnificent sex was inherently growth-enhancing, life-affirming and life-altering. (Note: We did specifically ask about the impact of optimal sexual experiences on a variety of things; however, the transformative effects of magnificent sex seemed to be woven into the fabric of the experience.) As one woman explained, "I don't think those experiences by their very nature can be anything less than transformative." Or as another said, "Something opens up that had been closed before." Some talked about experiencing alternate realities, trance states or "achieving a kind of a high" during magnificent sex. Others compared their best sexual experiences to their experiences during deep meditation. One woman said that magnificent sex "leaves you feeling bigger than you were before you started", while another stated that magnificent sex "can change you, can make you more than you are." One older woman said that she only started having magnificent sex in midlife, and described her experience of discovery:

> It was a door that I did not know existed and when I saw it for the first time, I *rushed* through it and felt like I had come home for the first time and it changed everything for me. It was a language that I spoke fluently the first time I heard it.

One man described the transformation he experienced as a result of magnificent sex:

> It changed the borders of my known universe. Like knocked them down, and I had to rethink – I don't know, not rethink – it re-contextualized all of my yearnings for a better world, my feeling of the commonness of humanity, my sense that our job on earth is to continue the work of creation every day in our lives.

This component is one of the reasons that we need to talk about magnificent sex. It's not frivolous – it can be life-altering. People talked about the benefits that it brought into their lives, the changes that it wrought. Sex is not just some bonus activity in life. It can define who we are, where we're going and what we're capable of becoming. We do not usually talk about transcendence and transformation in the world of clinical psychology, even though this may be exactly what people are yearning for.

Conclusion: The Components Are Universal – the Particulars Are Unique

"Great sex" in no way resembles the media stereotypes. It cannot be found by following pop culture advice for tips, tricks and techniques. On the contrary, in order to find optimal sexual experiences one must look within. If anything, participants taught us that rather than worrying about setting new bars for magnificent sex unattainably high, they highlighted the need to redefine "sex" per se.

People also invited us to contend with the issue of "risk". Couples therapists in general and sex therapists in particular tend to talk about keeping relationships emotionally safe and about keeping sex safe from the risks of unwanted pregnancy and sexually transmitted infections. We discuss the risks of emotional vulnerability but fail to consider the risks of erotic stagnation. In other words, we rarely consider the kinds of risks that are necessary for creating the calibre of sex worth wanting. We will return to this theme throughout this book.

Magnificent sex may involve those moments of deep connection in which both lovers are psychologically and sexually accessible, engaged and responsive to whatever lies deep within. In a context of safety and trust, lovers may risk further self- and other exploration of hidden erotic potentials.

Given the commonalities in extraordinary lovers' reports, are we to picture magnificent sex as having a certain uniformity? Are all optimal sexual experiences alike? Well, they all contain the same eight components but each experience is unique. How is this possible? Picture a recipe for chocolate chip cookies. They all contain the same basic ingredients: chocolate chips, eggs, flour, butter, baking soda, vanilla, sugar, brown sugar and maybe a pinch of salt. The recipe is necessary but not sufficient to bake up a batch of cookies that tastes just right to fit a particular mood. For one thing, one can always tailor or add extra ingredients, from extra-large chocolate chunks to different nuts. Even if two bakers began with identical ingredients, one could spoon them out in different sizes and bake them at different temperatures for different durations. One places

Ingredients
chocolate chips
eggs
flour
butter
baking soda
vanilla
sugar
brown sugar
salt

The Components are Universal – the Particulars are Unique

her cookies in the oven at 425° for 10 minutes and creates cookies that snap in one's fingers and crunch in one's mouth. Another places her cookies in the oven at 350° for 6 minutes and creates soft and chewy cookies. A third places her cookies in the oven at 375° for 8 minutes, resulting in cookies that are crunchy on the outside but are also moist, melt-in-your-mouth treats. It all depends on what would make your mouth water at the moment.

So what kind of special treat do you crave right now?

The Minor Components (or the Physical Aspects of Optimal Sexual Experiences)

One of the more striking and unexpected findings was how little the physical aspects of sex seemed to matter for magnificent sex. The people we interviewed compared their magnificent sexual experiences with many other, great, non-sexual activities such as eating a sumptuous dinner, riding motorcycles and playing an instrument. The physical side of optimal sexual experiences was mentioned by far fewer participants and was not emphasized to the same degree as the major components (e.g., communication, connection, being embodied). This is noteworthy because we specifically asked about a number of sex acts. Their answers were, as always, highly nuanced and complex. In this section, we will review the role of these minor components: lust and attraction; physical pleasure and intensity; and sex acts, particularly, intercourse and orgasm.

Lust, Attraction and Chemistry

The role of lust, chemistry and attraction in magnificent sex was touched on by several individuals, but these aspects were never emphasized to the same degree as were other aspects of optimal sexual experiences. As one person explained, "I believe it's partly just, quote unquote, chemistry or spark, but it's not entirely that." Another woman talked about the importance of connection over attraction:

> I think attraction helps if you're trying to create great sex. I don't, however, think it's ultimately necessary and it's all preference, it's all a bias. If you put a blindfold on me and hook me up with a . . . I don't know, a fat, brown Buddha from Tibet, his energy would

be amazing. I wouldn't ever need to see that he was bald and wearing orange, my least favorite colour, it's how he would feel.

Actually, this idea came up most frequently when we asked questions con-
cerning the three greatest sexual experiences of their lives. Many identified
the desire and attraction they feel for their partners and the strong mutual
lust or chemistry within their relationships as common elements across
their best experiences. "Overcome with desire" is how one man worded it.
A woman said, "In each of those encounters a component of, 'Oh my God!
If I go another minute without my hands on you, I shall simply cease to be.'"
Another man described one of the best parts of the experience for him:

> There's a point when I'm with someone who, uh, I know that
> whatever we're doing is going to lead to a sexual encounter and
> that is, it's a *delicious* part – I don't know quite how else to describe
> it – it's that point when you know that the casual kissing and the
> caressing, all that, is actually going to lead to having, uh, making
> sexual love. And that's, that's the first great sex moment is when
> the mouth goes dry, the knees get a little bit weak and there's this
> tingling in my groin.

Many said that feelings of attraction, desire and lust needed to be mutual, but
others mentioned only the importance of feeling desired themselves. A male
sex therapist believed that it was absolutely crucial for women to feel desired
but that it was not as important for men. "I think women are much more
turned on and satisfied by their partner's volcano-like desire than the man
is. The man is more likely to be turned off by that." This idea is common in
the sex therapy literature (see Meana, 2010) but was not reflected among our
(other) participants. Another man explained the joy he derived from the desire
he felt for his partner: "I think one of my favorite parts of interacting with
her is just adoring her body and watching her feel desired and appreciated,
and sexualized in ways that she never thought of sexualizing herself before."
Again, this stands in stark contrast to pop culture narratives around
"great sex". Sex scenes in movies, television shows and romance novels tend
to emphasize attraction and passion that characters feel for one another
(Ménard & Cabrera, 2011). And yet, the people we spoke to universally
focused on other contributors. As one man said:

> And sometimes it's folks that I'm not terribly attracted to, and/
> or that we're not feeling particularly passionate about each other

but we have great sex experience in a class together, or as part of group sex or, um . . . or in another way. But it's the willingness to be there and to take a risk.

This may be important for couples who are struggling with low desire, or even for couples who get along well and describe themselves as best friends but who wonder where their passion went over the years.

Physical Pleasure and Intensity

Many people we interviewed thought that feeling intense pleasure and high levels of arousal and build-up all contribute to making a sexual encounter magnificent. Magnificent sex usually involves a sense of great physical satisfaction, gratification and release, and sometimes even ecstasy. One older man said that during his greatest sexual experiences, "I am able to pull back into just pure sensual pleasure." Another person said:

> I felt pleasure to the point of just floating almost without a body at the end of it, to where I couldn't do any more and was just so totally satisfied and happy, couldn't get that smile off my face.

An older man described the "utter feeling of total satisfaction" that characterized magnificent sex for him.

Many reported that intensity is a crucial contributor to making a sexual experience magnificent. Some felt that intensity helps to differentiate between satisfying or good sexual experiences and amazing sexual experiences: During magnificent sex, every moment is experienced more deeply and strongly. "The feeling of physical, erotic, romantic connection was beyond belief" is how one man described this type of sex. An older man explained, "I think in great sex there is a degree of intensity and gratification that goes beyond just, just what you might call good sex." One person compared the difference between good and great sex to the Richter scale, saying, "It's an extreme to which one gets off."

Those who did mention this component specifically stated that great physical sensation on its own is insufficient to experience great sex and is secondary in importance to other components. As one person explained, "I think that great technique without . . . an emotional connection might be good but I don't think it's going to be – at least for me – it's not going to be great." Some said that great physical sensation is a more important characteristic of "hot" sex, which they defined as qualitatively different from "great" sex. The experience of intensely pleasurable physical sensation during magnificent sex was presented as an afterthought by several individuals, who had forgotten to mention earlier in the interview that magnificent sex "feels really, really good".

Sex Acts

Our sex therapist colleagues suggested that we include a question about the role of particular sex acts in our interview, but most extraordinary lovers remarked that the question is irrelevant for understanding what makes sex magnificent. Although participants sometimes divulged their preferences or the acts they enjoyed, no one singled out a specific sex act as being crucial for magnificent sex. Many went out of their way to point out that even though optimal sexual experiences are very physically pleasurable, they do not necessarily involve special stimulation techniques or sexual positions achievable only by Cirque du Soleil acrobats. An older man downplayed the importance of positions saying, "What counts is the joining of minds and bodies at the right time. It's a mind affair."

However, the notable exception was that many people mentioned kissing. Frequent kisses, prolonged kisses and deep kisses were all mentioned. One person defined kissing as "one of the most erotic exercises possible."

Intercourse

We did not originally have a question about intercourse/penetration until one of our early sex therapist participants suggested it. The overwhelming majority of extraordinary lovers told us that intercourse was irrelevant, inconsequential and/or unnecessary for optimal sexual experience. As one man put it:

> I mean it's just, you know, one way of being sexual but, I don't think in order to have great sex you have to be having intercourse and I don't think that having intercourse means you're going to have great sex.

Intercourse (whether penile/vaginal or anal intercourse) is just one of many activities that might or might not happen during an optimal sexual experience. Most told us that they had had magnificent sex both with and without intercourse. Quite a few described it as overrated or problematic because it could lead to an unnecessary focus on the genitals at the expense of other more important aspects. Several told us that they enjoyed intercourse and that it was fun but continued to de-emphasize its importance. One older man said:

> There needs to be a crossing of the boundary in a physical way but it doesn't have to be necessarily going inside someone. It can be going between them or a, wrapping up around or being wrapped up around by them. So it's a matter more of uh, kind of a blurring of the, of the strict boundaries but it doesn't have to include insertive behaviour.

That being said, a few people told us that it was one of their favorite activities or that it was special in some way to them. One man said that he thought, "It's a *beautiful* thing to be able to join physically with another body." An older woman said, "For me, it's very important because I want that much connection . . . intercourse itself is really important for me to feel bonded with my partner and to really feel like we are one, wonderful, sexy body." Another man explained, "There is a level of connection that you get when you do intercourse that's different."

Orgasm

Every month, *Cosmopolitan* and *Men's Health* promise their readers bigger orgasms, better orgasms or more orgasms (Barker, Gill & Harvey, 2018; Lavie-Ajayi & Joffe, 2009; Ménard & Kleinplatz, 2008). This fixation on orgasm, perhaps more surprisingly, is also evident in the academic literature. Masters and Johnson (1966) considered it to be the climax in their Human Sexual Response Cycle model, as did Kaplan. Most of the sexual dysfunctions listed in the *DSM* (that is, the *Diagnostic and Statistical Manual of Mental Disorders*) relate to orgasm in some way – reaching orgasm too quickly (premature ejaculation), too slowly (delayed ejaculation) or not at all (anorgasmia), or having body parts that will not cooperate in the production of orgasm (erectile dysfunction).

In response to questions on the role of orgasm in optimal sexual experience, the replies fell into a few distinct categories. A small minority of individuals felt that orgasms were an important and necessary contributor to magnificent sex. As one woman said, "Orgasm will tip me over into that moment of extended ecstatic connection with the universe which is what I really think is the peak of the experience." Another woman explained:

> I think it's pretty important. Although, I am not unlike, uh, many other women in believing strongly that I can have a really good

sexual experience without having an orgasm. I think in order for it to be great, it would have to, um, include losing myself enough to be able to reach that height of excitement and then to release it. So kind of that unconscious place, you know, where you just give it up during the orgasm, you know, that inevitability place where you're no longer thinking.

Even the people who felt that orgasm was necessary for magnificent sex also acknowledged that they had had optimal sexual experiences without orgasms. One woman said, "It's not a necessary feature of great sex, it's just so commonly a part of great sex that maybe I don't do well to separate them." One man said:

I don't think they are 100% absolutely necessary, um, but I think that, uh, if you're going to, you know, in the great sex in the world that probably about 99% of the time, they do involve an orgasm, at least one.

A few talked about the peak intensity, merger, loss of control and loss of boundaries. One woman explained that orgasms did not define magnificent sex but might relate to, "The highest end of the continuum where physiology and emotionality and relationship stuff all lines up together."

By far, the most common response was some version of "it's a bonus". Orgasms were wonderful, orgasms were delightful, orgasms were pleasurable but not necessary or sufficient. Several people talked about having non-linear models of magnificent sex: Rather than considering orgasm as the "grand finale" of an encounter, orgasms were just one more sexual act in the mix. One woman defined magnificent sex as, "a way more fluid and amorphous thing than an orgasm."

A few said that orgasms were irrelevant and unnecessary for magnificent sex. One man explained, "An orgasm always probably feels nice, but it's hardly, you know, a quasi-religious experience or calms your soul or makes you feel automatically closer to somebody else."

Gender Differences

A few people said that orgasms were probably necessary for men to define a sexual encounter as great but not for women. We heard this primarily from both male and female sex therapists but also occasionally from others we interviewed. Quite a few participants said that they did not personally need to have an orgasm in order for sex to be optimal but felt that their partners did. One sex therapist explained, "Sometimes, you know, the satisfaction of being with your partner and experiencing your *partner's* orgasm for a male or a female can be sufficient." One man we interviewed said, "It's her letting me participate in hers, her letting me hold her and be with her while she has them." A few people said that they did not mind if their partners did not have an orgasm as long as it was clear that they were satisfied. As one man said, "Orgasm needs to be communicated about or at least attended to."

3

MYTHS AND REALITIES OF MAGNIFICENT SEX

From Media Stereotypes and Beyond

In the course of the interviews, we were confronted repeatedly by the contrast between common assumptions and myths about sexuality as opposed to the realities of magnificent sex. There are many myths about sex, and about "great sex" in particular. In the absence of solid, research-based evidence, speculation, guesswork and anecdotes flourish like weeds in the popular media.

The goal of this chapter is to uproot a few of these more pernicious dandelions and to contrast them with some lessons from the extraordinary lovers we had interviewed. We will review some common, often unarticulated myths and juxtapose them with the realities of what sex can be. The "antidotes" are helpful enough to warrant considerable attention. Several of them will be explored more deeply in Part III. (For example, the myth that sex should be "natural and spontaneous" will be contrasted with the reality of extraordinary lovers' preparations which contribute to the creation of magnificent sex as elaborated in Chapter 5.)

The myths to be examined are drawn from media portrayals of "great sex" as well as reactions when we presented our research. In many cases, extraordinary lovers themselves brought up these myths specifically in order to debunk them. "These are the kind of stupid ideas I had to let go in order to be able to have truly great sex", was the message reported endlessly.

By contrast, what lessons can be learned from those who experience magnificent sex, even if they have been marginalized, especially the elderly (as well as those who are disabled or chronically ill, and members of sexual minority groups), and are not typically considered role models for "great sex"?

Why Do These Myths Matter and How Are They Relevant for Magnificent Sex?

Before entering into a discussion of the myths themselves, two of the most important lessons should be introduced in order to appreciate the adverse impact of common beliefs on normative sexuality and to demonstrate that there are alternatives to both the beliefs and their effects.

Great Lovers are Made – Not Born

Early in the interview process, at least in part to ascertain that participants were speaking about the same phenomenon, we asked them when they first experienced "great sex". We asked what brought about this first experience. In fact, we reworded the question repeatedly, in order to ensure that people would grasp and relay what we especially wanted to learn: At what age did you first experience "great sex"? What led to it? How did it come to happen? Did you acquire the capacity to bring it about? If so, how? Extraordinary lovers laughed at these questions and had vivid memories of their first optimal sexual experiences and what led to them.

Their first lesson is that great lovers are made – not born. Very few people had magnificent sexual experiences early on, although most of them had initially been rather impressed with their first, partnered sexual experiences, which they later came to understand as fairly naive assessments. Their collective narrative was: When I was in my teens, I thought getting laid was pretty great. When I hit my 20s, I thought having sex without my parents walking in was really great. In my 30s, I thought having sex without my kids walking in was great. But by the time I hit my 40s . . . I began to wonder, is that all there is? Is this as good as it gets? Was I willing to rock the boat? Was I willing to expose my vulnerabilities to get to really great sex? And that process of questioning was part of what led me to the calibre of sex that I first discovered in midlife.

As such, the most common period for first having what they currently considered "great" sex was in midlife. This discovery was rather demoralizing initially to the younger members of our audiences as we began to present this finding. Those in their 20s were asking, "Does this mean that I have to wait another 30-plus years before I can start having magnificent sex?" (The question as to whether anyone/everyone can enhance their sex lives and how they might do so is the focus of our final chapter.) It was in their 40s and 50s that people began to question their prior expectations, recognizing that they may have been too low. They also realized that if they wanted significantly better sex, it would require a serious investment of energy and effort. They recognized that if they were so inclined, they were better situated to pursue it than they were in their youth: They were clearer on what they wanted, better able to articulate and ask for it, and more skillful at negotiating.

Thus, participants' ability to demarcate the beginnings of "great" sex indicated a clear and distinct improvement in their sex lives as they reached midlife. They had developed the capacity for magnificent sex rather than having been "born that way".

The noteworthy message here is for individuals who may wish for optimal sexual experiences but have not had them yet. The operative word here is *yet*. Do not give up. Please consider learning from extraordinary lovers as to what elements they found helpful or even crucial in laying the groundwork for magnificent sex, but it may require entertaining some counter-intuitive ideas.

Overcoming Normative Sex Scripts

Almost without exception, those we spoke with reported that the first step towards magnificent sex entailed *unlearning* everything they had learned growing up about sex and sexuality. This necessitates overcoming prior shame, guilt, normative performance expectations and sex scripts (e.g., the ultimate end of sex should be penetration). It requires becoming less willing to settle for merely functional, but not necessarily fulfilling sex, when enacted primarily for the sake of maintaining relational harmony (Kleinplatz, 2011) – or avoiding a partner's disgruntled feelings. Improving one's sex life takes notable time, devotion and intentionality and cannot begin without acknowledging and discarding the restrictive sexual and heteronormative values and beliefs endemic in our society. As an older man stated emphatically:

> It really is important for people to become liberated from that sex negativity in order to continue and to attain better and better . . . "great sex". And that takes work . . . understanding where your hang-ups are, what your fears are and dealing with them . . . that you become free of them to be totally human. And that's one of

the reasons why sex for older people is better than for younger people. Younger people are still socialized into a mold of expectations that, um, are sometimes very difficult to overcome. I certainly was.

This message is especially important, although it meets with incredulity and perhaps even resistance in a North American social context. We are surrounded by open displays of sex and sexuality of every variety in the media, certainly in advertising and on the Internet. How could anyone argue that young people are still being socialized in a sex-negative environment? Here are a few leading questions which we will consider further in the chapter on clinical implications but which the reader may wish to reflect upon in the interim: If we actually do live in a sex-positive society, how is it that young (and old) adults still struggle to share their sexual desires and fantasies in the privacy of their bedrooms? How many North Americans are actually experiencing the calibre of sex they desire – and could this be linked to the high incidence of low sexual desire/frequency problems? If we are so comfortable dealing with sexuality, how is it that rates of sexually transmitted infections continue to rise among the young (Centers for Disease Control and Prevention, 2017, 2018; Choudhri et al., 2018a, 2018b, 2018c) and older adults (Emanuel, 2014), without a corresponding rise in sexual frequency (Twenge et al., 2016)? Does the public openness reflect cultural sexual comfort or reinforce private sexual discomfort and feelings of being defective (Kleinplatz, 2013)?

Some Myths and their Corresponding Realities – or Antidotes

Sex Should Be Natural and Spontaneous versus Magnificent Sex Involves Prioritizing and Being Deliberate

The notion that sex should be "natural and spontaneous" ranks among the most difficult assumptions to dislodge and among the most deleterious and dangerous to couples. It is so ubiquitous a hallmark for "great sex" as depicted in Hollywood movies that it has become a cliché. It is a contender for most damaging myth, encouraging individuals to devalue any sexual relations that took effort. In therapy, couples often rhapsodize about the honeymoon phase of the relationship, typically long before they married, when every time they saw each other they seemingly fell into each other's arms.

How does this compare to the descriptions of magnificent sex found among the extraordinary lovers? Among these individuals, magnificent sex might occasionally happen spontaneously but more commonly, it required considerable planning, prioritizing, being deliberate or, as one person summarized, "Great sex takes intentionality." That is, sex of this calibre does not simply "happen" but must be welcomed and invited into one's life. This requires considerable honesty about one's priorities. As one of our kinky participants stated, it is "important enough to really devote a lot of time". In other words, although in theory, when all the stars are in alignment sex might occasionally occur unexpectedly, in order to maximize the likelihood that magnificent sex might occur, one needed to create opportunity via one's choices. As an older man indicated:

> She and I . . . almost insisted on being with one another rather than with a bunch of other people. So we would not go to parties, we would not go to restaurants, would not attend concerts, we just want to be together. That's all, just the two of us. Anywhere.

The paradox here is that one cannot actually plan for optimal sexual experiences. One can, however, create the conditions in which magic *might* occur. Or as another woman worded it, "Having found great sex, it has become so important to me that, I'm clearer now about the, the lengths I'm willing to go to, to get it."

Magnificent Sex Requires Engaging in Intercourse versus "Every Point of Pleasure on the Circle Is an End in Itself"

In his book *Great Sex*, Michael Castleman (2004) describes a popular model of sex as, "A one-way drive downfield to the end zone of intercourse." This sequence of behaviours can be readily observed from the sex scenes depicted in most television shows, movies and romance novels. Each is usually written with the assumption that intercourse is the end-game, although certain behaviours are labelled as universally appealing and therefore strongly recommended (e.g., fellatio). The sequence is learned early and renowned among high school students joking about first base, second base, third base and eventually sliding in to home. This model also shows up in academic sex research. The most popular depictions of "normal sex" (e.g., Masters and Johnson's, Helen Singer Kaplan's) reflect some variation on the desire → "foreplay" →

intercourse → orgasm sequence of events. This can be seen in the write-up and organization of the sexual dysfunctions chapter of the *Diagnostic and Statistical Manual* (DSM, APA, 2013). Sexual dysfunctions are defined by the extent to which they disrupt this normal sequence (e.g., low sexual desire, erectile dysfunction, premature ejaculation, genital/pelvic pain impeding penetration, lack of orgasms).

Extraordinary lovers tend not to describe sex in a compartmentalized, linear way but describe a more free-flowing approach that involves a mix of connecting with one another, playing and communicating. An older man described his interactions with his partner, "Whenever I'm around my loved one, I'm having sex with her. It's *all* foreplay or it's *all* post-coital snuggling. I mean, it's always making love when we are intentionally together with the leisure to be together, it's lovemaking." Another commented, "It can be great if we have intercourse, it can be great if we [have] oral sex, it can be great if we're just making out." One woman remarked:

> Great sex I would say you have a circle, and every point on the circle is in itself, an end of pleasure, every point of pleasure on the circle is an end in itself. So intercourse can be one of those but it's not the *only* one of those.

Great Sex Involves "Date Night" Prepwork – Roses, Candles, Lingerie versus Tailor Preparation to the Needs of the Individuals and the Kinds of Sex They Anticipate

It's a cliché of romantic movies and novels that great sex involves extensive, time-consuming preparation. The bedroom in which this fictional great sex occurs has often been set with rose petals, candles, lingerie, chocolate-covered strawberries, champagne, soft music, etc.

Extraordinary lovers said that optimal sexual experiences do involve setting aside time and preparing their environment. However, no one believed that candles and rose petals were important or necessary ingredients. Rather, they emphasized the need to set up their environment so as to be congruent with the needs and interests of those involved. As one older woman stated:

> But the most important thing is that it not interfere with whatever kind of sex you wanted to have that day. So it could be quiet and private and comfortable with no interruptions for about four days

or it could be that the participants lose themselves in a room with other people in it or nearby. It depends what you want.

Some suggested that neat and tidy bedrooms might be conducive to magnificent sex. Another man suggested that indoor plumbing has been an important contributor to optimal sexual experiences on an historical level:

> I have no idea how people got, had great sex before there was indoor plumbing. You know, 'cause all this, you figure all this joyous sex stuff that, you know, this all, both people just bathed, and you know they're clean and they don't have fleas all over them and they're not cold and hot . . . so many amenities we take for granted.

Great Sex Requires Novelty versus Exploration and Familiarity versus Both Have Advantages

Pop culture recommendations on how to have wonderful sex often emphasize the importance of novelty: New positions, tricks, props and new locations are recommended in order to sustain a partner's interest. Buy some sexy lingerie, go away for the weekend, give sex toys a try or engage in "light" bondage. Recommendations of this type are often fairly narrow and suggest that consumers avoid anything that is too "out there" or "kinky".

By contrast, extraordinary lovers did not emphasize the importance of surprise and novelty. It was, however, important to approach sexual encounters and partners with an attitude of openness. One woman described her "novel" sexual encounters:

> There's always an element of, of new-ness or novelty, um, but not novelty in the, like, cheap plastic toy sense um novelty in the, 'I have never experienced this, thus it is a new experience and an unexpected one' sense.

Another woman talked about bringing a "sense of discovery and wonder" to sexual encounters with her long-term partners. One person explained why she and her partner engage in novel behaviours:

> I think couples – myself and my partner included – have little ways of bringing novelty, um, into our sexual experiences. And whether that's engaging in sex at a different time of day or whether it's ah, ah

trying a new technique or trying a sex toy or even just, um, talking during sex, um, it could be almost anything that is different from the way we did it most of the time, um I think adds an element of risk and excitement, it increases our interest, increases the odds that we'll want to do it again, um, it increases our sense of safety in the relationship if it goes well and safety in the relationship then increases the odds that we can seek more novelty together.

Many waxed lyrical about the benefits of familiarity and building on the solid foundation of a long-term relationship. Or as a kinky man said, "With a familiar person, it's better because you have that bond, you have that trust, you got experience with each other." For such individuals, the emphasis was not on new sexual acts or props but on creating a context for revealing one another anew and in ever-deeper ways. Their focus was on the opportunity for self-exploration afforded in deeply intimate relationships. Or as a kinky woman reported, "Part of great sex too is that discovery process, that it never stops." That is, a balance is required between discovery and trust, which in turn creates an atmosphere rich with "anticipated surprise".

Great Sex Means Great Orgasms versus Orgasm Helps But Is Neither Necessary Nor Sufficient

The question that I [A.D.M.] encountered most frequently in describing this research to acquaintances, friends and family members was: "Great sex? Well, that's just great orgasms, isn't it?" There is a pervasive assumption in the general population, fuelled by media content, that great sex means great orgasms or possibly multiple orgasms or – even better – simultaneous, mutual orgasms.

Because of the prevalence of this idea, we specifically asked about the role of orgasm in bringing about magnificent sex. Most said that although orgasms were extremely pleasurable, they were neither necessary nor sufficient for magnificent sex. As one older man described the situation, "Orgasm doesn't guarantee it or prevent it." An older man described the role of orgasms in his greatest sexual experiences:

> I think it is, um, part of the experience, not the best or the only, um, part. I think, um, uh, perhaps there's a physical intensity, uh, and maybe even an emotional intensity where that feels, uh, there's a peak sense of being vulnerable, of being out of control of um . . . Okay, I think the sensation is all, kind of all over your

body, one time. Um, instead of, just kind of, different times and different parts of your body . . . I think about it as, as maybe a point where one, so to speak – not the most or the only but certainly it is a point where, um, couples, uh, allow their partner, um, in, uh, in terms of, giving to them in a very intense kind of way. So letting go. [pause] Sometimes I think of it as a, um, merging or a loss of boundaries, both emotionally and physically.

Several people talked about delaying their orgasms for hours on end in order to build arousal. As one woman reported: "The greatest sex experiences that I have had did not involve orgasm [but] involved *denial* of orgasm, or involved the *deliberate* holding back of orgasm, in order for the arousal or so forth." In the BDSM world, this pattern of heightening and savouring arousal is often referred to as "edging".

Great Sex Only Happens at the Beginning of a Relationship versus Magnificent Sex in Long-Term Relationships Requires *Not* Lowering Expectations Over Time

This myth was expressed by some sex therapists who participated in the study. The gist of this myth is that couples should lower their expectations: Great sex is what happens in the first year of a relationship but should not be expected thereafter except on special occasions (e.g., going on vacation, on anniversaries and birthdays). One sex therapist told us:

> My feeling is that that kind of intensity that occurs in the beginning of a relationship changes over time so that the greatness of the sex is less great in a long-term relationship. I don't think that one can maintain that kind of intensity that I described in the beginning [of the interview].

This idea seems to pervade the academic literature as well. Historically, there has been very little research on sex and sexuality among older people and those partnered for 20, 30 or more years and still less on sexual satisfaction within this group.

Certainly, some people said that magnificent sex was possible at the beginning of a relationship. A few singled out the high levels of passion and intensity that occur in the early stages of a new relationship, especially if desire had been spun out over a long period of time and gratification had been delayed. However, many emphasized that sex is likely to get *better* over time, provided that certain criteria are met. With experience, many found that they were less willing to settle for anything less than what they really wanted. They talked about valuing sex, both as individuals and within the relationship. They spoke of prioritizing sex in their lives and making time for it. As one older man stated, "People who understand that sexuality in a long-term relationship involves effort. I'm not going to say work, but effort." Within their relationships, extraordinary lovers said that they communicated extensively with their partners and explored together. They explained the importance of ongoing learning and discovery. One man explained the changes in his marriage over time:

> Like no matter how much you know someone, things change over time. Um, the, the way that my partner and I have sex after 17 years looks very different from, or, you know, we do very different things. Uh, you know, like for example, within the, within the general category of oral sex, the things that we like have changed over time. So, yes, I mean, they may both look similar to the outsider but to us, it's clearly very different. Um, and so being able to recognize that and not take it personally.

Many talked about the importance of willingness, openness to experience and making adaptations to changes over time. They emphasized that this takes courage, daring, boldness and creativity. It is enhanced by the freedom to take chances without worrying about making mistakes; that freedom comes from the growing trust in a relationship over time. Many people said that they were surprised to find themselves having better sex later in the relationship than they did at the outset.

Sex Deteriorates with Age versus Magnificent Sex Benefits from Experience and Maturity

In Western culture, the sexual practices and interests of older individuals have often been marginalized. Older characters who still talk about sex or engage in sexual activities are frequently the butt of cringe-oriented, sitcom jokes. Older individuals are not represented in advertising, unless the advertiser is peddling pills to treat erectile dysfunction. If older people are having sex at all, it is assumed that they must be experiencing one (or more) sexual dysfunctions (e.g., low desire, lack of lubrication, erectile dysfunction, pain). The unfortunate consequence of these representations is that the elderly themselves may hold limiting self-stereotypes (DeLamater & Koepsel, 2015).

Both the older individuals and the sexual minority members reported that over time, their definitions of magnificent sex and what it takes to get there grew increasingly demanding. As an older man reported, "It's like somewhere in there, I hit another gear and saw possibilities that I didn't think about before, wasn't aware of missing anything. But I found other, I found more keys on the keyboard." A woman reported:

> I think that as I have had more experiences, and I have been more open in talking about sexual experiences with my partners and others who are willing to talk, um, that it has helped me open my mind to possibilities and a broader interpretation of, um, sex in general. Um, I understand, um, that sex in general can have a broader definition than the full missionary, you know, penetration of a woman's vagina and I think that I was naive enough to think as I entered my first long-term relationship, which was with my husband, um, that, uh, there were certainly any number of positions and any number of things that could go on during an act of intimacy, but I still was fairly narrow in scope in terms of, um, the depth of what could happen, in terms of emotional connection, and the spiritual connection, and energy exchange and so on. That's evolved over time and I think that that's true for anybody, that it takes a certain maturity to be able to, um, tap into those kinds of introspection and reflections.

Many expressed surprise and delight upon discovering that sex can improve with experience and maturity. As one older man said, "Well, I was not as good a lover as I was 19 to 40 as I was thereafter and I probably am a better lover today than when I was 40 . . . ." He said that he and his partner looked forward to what the next 10 or 20 years might bring.

Many older individuals said that as they mature, magnificent sexual experiences become less about performance, technique and orgasms, and more focused on the relational and spiritual components of the experience. Quite a few said that when they were younger, "great sex" was any sex, and it tended to be very goal-oriented. This changed with experience, as an older man reported:

> Young people are more performance and, and, uh . . . [sighs] They're just too anxious. Older people have more of an understanding for what it takes to join, like for minds to join and what it takes to control your mind to enjoy great sex. I mean, I think back to myself, I was 15 years old the first time I made love to

a friend of mine who I actually went to grade school together with. And [laughs] was that great sex? Absolutely not. Did I have great sex before I was 20 years old? Well in my own mind I did because I met somebody and we had sex. That was not great sex. We were young, we were anxious, we were quick. No. Sex comes with maturity. It doesn't matter that you're necessarily mature at 25 or mature at 55, it's something that gradually increases with age. Sex becomes better and better with time.

Another person explained the transition in thinking about great sex over time:

> So, the big difference is in realizing, when you're young, sexuality is much more about what's physical. I think as you get older, again it's a finite number of tabs and a finite number of slots and the things you really want to do, you know, you want to try this and try that and see if you can have a three-way . . . Whatever, you know, little, um, experiences you wanted to have on your list, as you get older you kind of check those things off your list and at the point that you've checked a lot of them off, you realize that it has to do with transcendence and awareness and acuity and clarity, um, so it becomes really different when you're older. And personally, I think, extremely, um, a lot better in a certain way.

Older lovers reported that being open to learning new things about themselves, their partners and sex itself had resulted in overall personal growth and development. As a kinky woman said, "I think they have to be willing to try things and, not afraid, not closed down. I think that you have to be okay with making mistakes." Their continued questioning and re-evaluation throughout their lives had led to greater comfort with themselves in general and with their sexuality. Or as an older man in a very long-term marriage explained, "You've been through so many ups and downs that you know you're going to come out of it OK."

Great Sex Is for Beautiful, Able-Bodied People versus Chronic Illness and Disability Do Not Necessarily Preclude Optimal Sexual Experience

At the beginning of each interview, in the course of collecting demographic data, we asked everyone about their health and ability/disability status. The majority self-defined as healthy and able-bodied. This was illuminating because as we would occasionally discover in the course of the interviews, some of these same people would be described objectively in medical terms as seriously ill. For example, one man who had initially described himself as healthy and able-bodied interrupted an interview to say he "just" needed to get his oxygen and would be right back. He returned and reassured us that he was set to continue – it was simply that he had COPD (i.e., chronic obstructive pulmonary disease). It was a turning point in the research. We were puzzled but later came to realize that one element of how extraordinary lovers approached life in general was with a *joie de vivre* that also pervaded their sexuality. As an older man noted:

> Someone who looks on themselves as being somehow broken . . . need not map to any kind of externally-defined disability . . . It never struck me as being a defining issue in terms of sexual engagement, sexual passion . . . *If there were a disability that restricts one's access to sexual fulfillment, I would say it was a disability of the energy or the imagination.*

Similarly, some were disabled, chronically ill or had cared for and outlived partners who had been sick. The medical conditions they reported included heart disease, strokes, multiple sclerosis, various types of cancer (and their treatments, for example, mastectomies, hysterectomies, prostatectomies, etc.), HIV, epilepsy, arthritis, spinal stenosis, hearing loss and incontinence. They would surely have been an obstacle to normal sexual functioning. However, they did not prevent optimal sexual experience. As an older woman said, "You can always have sex in a new form." As one older, kinky man described:

> I'd say that my life is better than it's ever been, in spite of increasing levels of disability, because there's a lot more love in it and there's a lot more, you know, uh, kind of energy and, um, I just feel better about myself and about other people.

As another noted, "With the right partner, I don't need Viagra or Cialis. Without the right partner, drugs won't help!"

In some cases, sex only became magnificent after prior sexual options became impossible; the experience of disability caused the individual to set aside assumptions and preconceptions about sex, which helped open the door to magnificent sexual experiences. An older, kinky man commented, ". . . a lot of barriers to great sex for able-bodied people [occur] as they hold themselves to standards that get in the way of open-mindedness and experimentation".

This perspective on life itself from among individuals with disabilities is worthy of further research that goes well beyond the domain of sexology. Please keep these extraordinary lovers and what they have to teach us in mind as we continue to consider what makes for magnificent sex. In essence, they are forcing us not only to grapple with conventional images of who "sex is for" but more importantly, they are challenging us to re-envision "sex" per se.

Extraordinary lovers indicated that none of these elements is necessary for optimal sexual experiences. Many spontaneously volunteered that they did not consider themselves or their partners conventionally, physically attractive by mainstream standards. One man explained how his thinking about the role of attractiveness and optimal sexual experiences had changed over his life:

> I think, you know, although your body changes and your, you get a little wrinkled, if you still have enthusiasm, uh, you can still be attractive to people. When I turned 40 I thought, 'Oh this is it, I'll never get laid again.' But that turned out not to be true and then when I turned 50 I thought the same thing and again it turned out not to be true and then it happened again when I was 60 and when I was 70. And I'm still having great sex and I think that's really quite wonderful.

Some said that they or their partners were overweight or obese; these same individuals often said that optimal sexual experiences had gone a long way to curing them of hang-ups related to body image.

The interviews with older, chronically ill and disabled individuals teach that magnificent sex in no way resembles functional sex. *The good news is that sexual functioning is not necessary for magnificent sex.* That means that aging, chronic illness and disability do not necessarily preclude and may even be an asset towards optimal sexual development. *The bad news is that sexual functioning is not sufficient for magnificent sex* (Kleinplatz, 2010, 2016; Ménard et al., 2015). Having a hard penis (or two) or a wet vagina will allow for adequate sexual functioning but they are no guarantee of magnificent sex.

Great Sex Can Only Occur within the Context of Loving, Long-Term, Monogamous Relationships versus Magnificent Sex Comes in Many Forms of Consensually Non-Monogamous Relationships

The sex therapists we interviewed often gave very different answers from the participants who had actually experienced magnificent sex. One of the major assumptions made by the sex therapists in this study was that optimal sexual experiences could only happen within the context of a loving, monogamous, long-term relationship. No allowances were made for having optimal sexual experiences with friends, casual partners, play partners or any type of consensually non-monogamous or polyamorous configuration.

Some individuals had only had optimal sexual experiences with one person and did not believe that it was possible for them to have magnificent sex with someone else, although many were careful to explain that this was only true for themselves and not necessarily for others. Others were openly and consensually non-monogamous (e.g., swinging, polyamory) but had only had magnificent sex with their primary partner, while others had optimal sexual experiences across partners. Their accounts were verified when we interviewed partners in the same relationship back-to-back, with no opportunity for them to speak with one another between interviews. For example, when we asked how and when they came to be consensually non-monogamous, each partner described the same timing and sequence of events, as in the case of a married couple, who each separately specified, "Great sex began 12 years ago . . . when we went poly." A few specified that their swinging experiences were "hot" but not "great". However, many people reported that magnificent sex can be experienced within the context of different types and durations of relationship as long as certain elements are in place, such as trust, safety, caring, communication and respect. Sometimes these relationships were within a polyamorous context. Sometimes people were talking about friendships involving a sexual component.

A Serendipitous Lesson: Group Similarities and Differences in Optimal Sexual Experiences

Pop culture stereotypes would have us believe that men and women feel, think and behave in different but complementary ways when it comes to sex. The quintessential examples are John Gray's bestsellers of the 1990s, which claim that men are from Mars and women are from Venus. More recently, evolutionary sexology claims that men and women are designed to be different sexually for the sake of the propagation of the species. In any event, the stereotypes suggest that for men, any sex is great sex. Men are expected to focus on conquering many sexual partners and check off a variety of different experiences (e.g., anal intercourse, threesomes). According to traditional, gendered sexual scripts, for women, sex can only be great in a committed relationship, and would usually involve extensive foreplay, mind-blowing orgasms given to her by her skilled partner and cuddling afterwards (which their male partners are expected to abhor). Theoretically, these differences are thought to lead to problems and dysfunction unless men and women learn what the other sex "really wants in bed".

Gender/sex research in the academic world has often reinforced these stereotypes by focusing on the differences in sexual attitudes and behaviours between men and women. However, many studies have found that supposed gender differences in areas such as level of sexual desire, frequency of masturbation, frequency of fantasies and frequency of "one-night stands" are inconsistent at best (Peterson & Hyde, 2010). Some studies have found gender differences in levels of sexual satisfaction and well-being but most have not. The results from one study showed that perceived differences in sexual behaviours between men and women are negligible in an experimental condition where participants were led to believe that false answers on questionnaires could be detected by researchers (Alexander & Fisher, 2003). It would appear that many participants in that study felt the need to respond in a way that was consistent with gender stereotypes rather than disclose their actual behaviours and attitudes.

However, in our research, an unexpected picture of male-female and other group differences – or lack thereof – emerged (Kleinplatz, Ménard, Paradis et al., 2013). As indicated in Chapter 1, phenomenologically-oriented research methodology does not allow for testing of differences between groups. We had undertaken discovery-oriented (i.e., What is magnificent sex?) rather than hypothesis-testing research (i.e., Does optimal sexual experience differ between men and women? The old versus the young? The "vanilla" versus the kinky?). Yet as soon as we began to distribute masked transcripts – that is, transcripts devoid of all identifying and demographic information for ethical reasons – we began to notice a pattern among the other members of our research team. We [P.J.K. and A.D.M.] were the only ones who knew which interview transcript came from which sort of participant and could not help but notice that our fellow team members' guesses as to who was whom were erroneous (e.g., male versus female). By 2013, the similarities among the experiences of extraordinary lovers became undeniable. With sincerest apologies to our fellow phenomenologists, we felt compelled to publish our observation that our research team members found men and women, the young and the old, vanilla and kinky participants indistinguishable (Kleinplatz, Ménard, Paradis et al., 2013).

That is, in our research, no major differences were noted between the responses of men and women. As one participant explained, "I think probably when we reach that level of calling something great or excellent or optimal, I think probably most gender differences would disappear." Another woman described her partner's experience: "I've seen his face and that's a good mirror to what I'm feeling at the time." Or as one older man stated:

> It's probably the most *peer* sex that I've ever had. We have – our particular, um, uh, sexual relationship dynamics that we've developed, um, right from the start but ultimately what goes on is there's a great *peerness* that, that sex between us becomes genderless. That's never happened to me. It's fantastic.

Many more differences were observed among men and women than between them.

Most participants, regardless of sex, touched on all of the major components of magnificent sex. Great sex did not mean "great orgasms" for men and "great relationships" for women. Both men and women talked about exploration; both men and women talked about the spiritual component of optimal sexual experiences; both men and women talked about having sex in a committed relationship; both men and women talked about having sex with friends/play partners. In terms of the contributors to magnificent sex, each person's route up the mountain was unique. Men did not focus on skills, technique and variety; women did not focus on the relational contributors. Again, research team members could not distinguish between interviews conducted with men versus interviews with women.

Presumed differences between the sexual experiences of men and women such as men's higher desire for sex, men's emphasis on the genitals and orgasm and women's emphasis on the relationship did not appear in studying optimal sexual experience (Kleinplatz, Ménard, Paradis et al., 2013).

Although the research team had difficulty distinguishing the transcripts of those individuals recruited on the basis of their age and experience from those recruited on the basis of their inclusion in a marginalized group, they could reliably identify those interview transcripts belonging to sex therapists. When we asked our team members what led them to remark, "Oh no! Not another sex therapist!" – and indeed, they were correct about the origin of these transcripts in every instance – they opined that these transcripts were distinctive: The sex therapist interviewees believed that great sex fades after the first couple of years of the relationship; they focused on the need for normal sexual functioning in order to have sex at all; and they rarely mentioned the importance of playfulness for optimal sexual experience. In summary, as we wrote in our 2013 article:

> Strikingly, the descriptions of optimal sexuality were nearly universally identical among the first two participant groups; that is,

across men and women, older married people, and lesbian, gay, bisexual, and transgender (LGBTQ) or 'kinky' participants; however, the sex therapists were conspicuous outliers. Even though five raters in the research team were blind as to the demographic characteristics of the participants, raters consistently and accurately detected the sex therapists' transcripts and conceptions as undeniably and markedly different.

Lessons from Extraordinary Lovers: Re-visioning Sexuality

What stands out here is that myths surrounding "great sex" are not only erroneous but that the reality as described by extraordinary lovers is more inspiring. Optimal sexual experiences can be found among a wide array of individuals and lovers. However, approaching the capacity for magnificent sex will require discarding many of the constricting fallacies that are still being perpetuated. That may require adjusting our mindsets but will open the expanse of possibilities for magnificent sex to many more of us.

PART III

PART III

WHAT LEADS TO MAGNIFICENT SEX?

Contributing Factors

Our research had begun to shed light on the nature of magnificent sex (Kleinplatz, Ménard, Paquet et al., 2009). However, in the same way that it is not possible to look at a Rénoir painting or an Olympic-calibre athletic performance and understand how to recreate it oneself, it does not seem possible to bring about optimal sexual experiences merely by understanding what they look like. In order to do so, it was necessary to identify, explore and define the contributors or facilitating factors of magnificent sex.

It was important to ensure that everyone had the same phenomenon in mind when we inquired about optimal sexual experiences. That meant we had to ask the same questions in several different ways (which is the norm in phenomenological interview methodology) to get as close as we could to understanding magnificent sex. Therefore, we asked about good sex, very good sex, great sex and the three best sexual experiences of our participants' lives. This procedure helped to ensure that people were on the same page across interviews when asked further questions about "great" or "the best" thereafter. In this next phase of our research, as we attempted to identify contributing factors to optimal sexual experiences, we began by confessing to participants that we were not even sure as to how to word the question, "What leads to magnificent sex?" We would then rephrase the question as, "What led *you* to great sex?" We would add, "When was the first time you had really great sex?" "What did you do to help bring this calibre of sex about?" "Did you *learn* how to have magnificent sex?" "Were you just lucky?" "Were you born lucky?" "How did it first come about?" "What made that happen?" "Did you do something in particular that led to it?" "Do you now do special things to make it happen?" "Can you plan for it?" "Is it something that people can *attain*?" "If so, how?" "If not, why not?"

Our goal for the next phase of this research was to learn what leads to magnificent sex. That meant we needed to identify the broadest possible range of contributors to optimal sexual experiences, such as the experiences, qualities, skills, etc. that help to bring about magnificent sex. In identifying the factors that lead to magnificent sex, our aim was to take the broadest possible stance on the subject. We were interested in factors that were relevant at any point across a person's lifetime (e.g., events / experiences that occurred in childhood, adolescence and early adulthood). We wanted to include contributors that were important before, during and after sexual encounters. We were interested in factors that contributed directly towards making a sexual experience magnificent or indirectly through their impact on some other factor. We wanted to consider factors that contribute to a specific aspect of optimal sexual experiences, as well as contributors to the *Gestalt* of optimal sexual experiences. Contributors might vary in their importance: Some might be desirable but not crucial, others might be necessary but not sufficient and still others might be absolutely critical. We wanted to include qualities of the individual that contributed to their having magnificent sex, qualities of the relationship(s) in which optimal sexual experience occurred and qualities related to the larger culture / environment that made magnificent sex possible. In short, any contributor that might in any capacity help to bring about magnificent sex was of interest to us.

In Part III, each chapter will describe one of the major contributing factors to optimal sexual experiences. Some pertain to the individual (e.g., being comfortable in one's body), while others pertain to the relationship (e.g., mutual trust). The temporal sequence is of interest: Some factors go all the way back to childhood (e.g., the nature of the sex education one received), while others are an enduring part of one's personality (e.g., *joie de vivre*) or of one's relationship (e.g., mutual empathy). Still other contributing elements occurred immediately prior to sexual relations, for example, taking a shower or ensuring that any interpersonal conflict had been resolved successfully. In addition, some of the factors occurred *during* sexual activities, including skills (e.g., self-awareness while connecting with the other), facilitating factors on the part of the individual during sex (e.g., letting go) and on the part of the couple (e.g., devoting themselves to one another in the moment).

In the final chapter of Part III, we will focus attention on the differences in emphases and pathways towards magnificent sex from one individual or couple to the next. That is, some highlighted their own states of mind as important contributors; others featured some quality of the relationship in order for the sex to be optimal; and still others emphasized some quality of the sex itself that enhanced the eroticism. More importantly, we discovered that particular sequences of individual and relational factors created different pathways for different individuals and couples. The complexity and uniqueness of these pathways requires particular attention for sex and couples therapists.

4
DEVELOPMENTAL FACTORS

Unlearning

For many, the first steps along the path towards optimal sexual experiences involved unlearning much of what they previously thought they knew about sex and sexuality. Many people had internalized negative, destructive or simply constricting messages during their earlier years. Some messages came from parents and family members; others were delivered by teachers, peers or media sources. One kinky man told us about the secret shame he carried around for many years:

> I started out adolescence with a huge, horrendous, horrible sexual perversion. So having had a sexual perversion was a big obstacle to being able to figure out how to unscramble all of this. I knew it was a perversion because I knew what everybody else thought, and I myself felt terrible about being, you know, something like having leprosy. How could I have good sex if I was a leper? And yet, what it is that turned me on and made my knees incredibly weak was something that you weren't supposed to want so.

Some singled out bad relationships and the partners who shamed them about their bodies or their sexual interests.

Early negative messages seemed to be a particular challenge for those who identified as LGBTQ from a young age, as well as for those whose sexual interests fell outside the mainstream (e.g., interests in kink, BDSM, polyamory).

Some people fully expected to be rejected or even shunned by lovers, friends and family if they were to be honest and authentic about who they were and what they wanted. Many told us that they had hidden those aspects of themselves away until middle age and sometimes later.

Some reported early experiences of sexual, emotional and/or physical abuse perpetrated by family members or early partners. A few also described sexual assaults that were often followed by unsupportive reactions from family, friends and/or professionals. The sadness, fear and despair were so clear and raw in their narratives, which makes the changes and the distance they covered even more extraordinary. These same people often expressed amazement and astonishment at how far they had come since their terrible beginnings.

Even for those who had escaped harsh, negative messages or traumatic sexual events, the messages conveyed by mainstream Western media regarding sex, sexuality and great sex are often problematic. The focus on rigid gender roles, a restricted range of "appropriate" activities and an overwhelming emphasis on the physical aspects of sex were challenging for many people. One woman described her concerns with conventional thinking about sex in society:

> A lot of the problems that I think people have . . . is the sense of shame and guilt and badness that we gather through our childhood by being told not to touch ourselves, not to look at sexual pictures or have sexual thoughts. To, you know, somehow de-sex ourselves until the age of 18 when you suddenly have permission to go out and use a part of your body and of your being and your mind that you've actually had since birth.

It is important to recognize the variety of detrimental experiences that these individuals described from their childhoods, adolescence and adulthood. Hardly anyone had a perfect, problem-free, sex-positive early life and yet all of them had found their way to amazing sexual experiences. Reaching magnificent sex may require overcoming a variety of challenges; interestingly, this had been possible for everyone that we interviewed. None of the problems described above is an automatic, immutable barrier to magnificent sex. In other words, for those who are interested in improving in their sex lives, we did not find any predetermined, fixed limitations that could not be managed. This is certainly encouraging news for those who feel excluded by mainstream narratives or for those who believe themselves to be broken or damaged beyond repair by early life experiences.

Letting Go and Overcoming

Before magnificent sex could be possible in their lives, extraordinary lovers had to let go, deconstruct or overcome the restrictive ideas about sex and themselves that had become embedded in their minds. It was necessary to wipe the slate clean in order to become the kind of people they needed to become and to develop the kind of relationships they needed for optimal sexual experiences to become possible. They described a process of comparing their sexual desires with mainstream standards, finding these standards to be lacking or limiting or simply irrelevant to them and choosing instead to pursue their authentic desires. When asked when it was that sex became magnificent, one woman replied, "Once I allowed myself the freedom to let it be what it could be, and I didn't continue to fall within societal definitions and expectations." Working through shame and guilt was a recurring theme and often represented an ongoing, sometimes lifelong process. An older man described his beliefs about the process of overcoming sex negativity:

> That takes work, that takes psychological work and self-evaluation and understanding where your hang-ups are, what your fears are and dealing with them and however that might happen so that you become free of them *to be totally human.*

The importance of letting go and overcoming was particularly true for those people who experienced a change in their life circumstances due to illness and injury. One man who had been diagnosed with a neurodegenerative disease explained his experience:

> I'm not even sure I had a definition of great sex until a few years ago. It's like, you know, there was sex and I don't think I would classify most of it as great . . . sometimes it would feel better than others, but I don't think I would have classified much of it as 'great sex' if somebody had asked. And then I sort of lost the ability to do that . . . After I was forced to accept that my previous definitions of sex weren't working, and just kind of gave up on trying to do that and became much more open to experimenting and communicating and responding to what [my wife] wanted . . . Sex was much more intense than it ever was before. Even though I still wasn't having erections or orgasms myself, the whole experience as a whole was, I thought, was much greater than anything I had back then.

The specific messages they had to overcome and the journeys taken towards challenging those and leaving them behind were deeply personal. Therefore, we cannot offer any blanket directive or advice that would be suitable for all readers (e.g., "Take a workshop!", "Go to therapy!", "Have sex with lots of people!"). Self-reflection is a critical piece of this process. However, for those who are willing to expend effort and who are actively interested in cultivating optimal sexual experiences, opportunities sometimes present themselves, for those who are open to them (see Chapter 7).

In some cases, meeting a special person triggered the process of letting go and overcoming negative messages. With the guidance and support of loving partners, it became possible to explore one's self and one's sexuality, and to discover and develop important personal qualities. Often, these relationships had long-since ended but the lovers still retained fond feelings and looked back on those experiences and those relationships with gratitude. One older woman told us how her first husband helped her overcome early negative messages:

> He allowed me to open up and blossom and encouraged me and, and was never ever critical. He was always saying to me things like, 'How could you be hurting anybody? This is so wonderful!' and it just started changing my attitude . . . He was so far advanced in his comfort with his own sexuality he just, you know, swept me up in it and helped me relax. It was wonderful.

Confronting and letting go of past experiences and messages may be difficult and to be clear, it is not necessary to overcome and resolve all barriers and challenges before magnificent sex becomes possible. Many people were clear that they still had concerns to work on, but their attitudes had changed. In many cases, they had become softer and gentler with themselves, abandoning the internalized voices of their harshest critics. One woman told us about her journey:

> Growing up, my dad, he wasn't a kind man and he would often tell me I was fat or I was ugly or I was worthless or anything like that. And I remember my partner telling me that one day I was going to see myself through his eyes, and I distinctly remember the day that I did. We had just had amazing sex and I got up and I went to the bathroom and I walked past the mirror and I saw this woman I didn't recognize.

In addition, optimal sexual experiences themselves could be corrective and healing. This sets up a kind of virtuous cycle – letting go and overcoming previous messages and experiences broadens and deepens one's capacity for optimal sexual experiences, which contain their own kind of teaching and healing powers to further the process of letting go and overcoming.

"Bien dans sa Peau": Comfort with Self

In our research team, we spent considerable time looking for just the right words to capture our participants' experiences. In this instance, it was research team member Nicolas Paradis, M.Ed., who found precisely the right expression for this element: "Bien dans sa peau", a French expression which means to feel at ease in one's own skin. (It is often helpful to be in a multi-lingual research team.)

Extraordinary lovers described the importance of developing greater comfort with themselves across all levels, physically, mentally and spiritually. Magnificent sex requires people to feel comfortable, embodied and grounded in themselves. One man described this phenomenon:

> I used to, many years ago, say that you could see someone and feel that they were comfortable inside their own bodies as they walked down the street. You could feel that they kind of occupied their bodies as opposed to they just happened to be in their body.

At the outset of the interviewing process, we asked everyone about the impact of magnificent sex on body image; however, many turned the question around, telling us that a good body image helps to bring about optimal sexual experiences. (Some people did acknowledge that magnificent sex helped them to feel good about their bodies, creating a positive feedback loop.) Some described themselves and their partners as being unselfconscious with regard to their bodies. As one man put it, "They're not afraid to show every body part they have." An older woman described the beginning of a romance that resulted in some truly magnificent sex: "He was just so comfortable in his body and so at ease and he just was so attractive to me for that . . . I started looking at him in a totally different light than I had been previously."

Comfort with their bodies (or that of their partners) was not based on mainstream standards of attractiveness (e.g., tall, thin, able-bodied). Many extraordinary lovers spontaneously remarked that neither they nor their partners would be judged attractive by conventional measures. A woman in her 40s described how and why her feelings of comfort with herself had improved over her life:

> At my current age, I am *way* more sexy than I was at . . . 29 or even at 18. My image of myself as a sexual being increases with time. Part of that was the positive feedback I got from my partners but

also part of it was being in an environment where I saw a lot of different body types naked. Being at dungeon parties, and being at different places where people would play naked and realizing that, you know, everybody has their little bumps and bulges and stuff but I would be looking at a woman and going, 'My God, she is sexy' and then realizing that classically, she's around 100 pounds overweight but she is still, you know, in my opinion, sexy. And that, you know, helped me realize that, you know, I had my own, you know, sex appeal.

Some people, especially among the older individuals, had undergone significant, life-changing illnesses or injuries (e.g., cancer and mastectomy, multiple sclerosis, emphysema) that had affected their appearance. Many in this group said that they felt better about their bodies at present, despite these changes, than they had when they were younger. Despite these challenges, most described a transition over time from a more negative view of self to a more compassionate, positive appraisal. An older woman, who had undergone a mastectomy, described the process for her:

I've gone from repression, self-loathing, shame into feeling like this glorious creature [laughs] that owns her own body . . . When I was nineteen or a younger woman, the last thing I would do is take off my clothes and let anybody see me, let alone see me without a right breast. I'm *very* comfortable with myself.

For most, comfort with self had developed slowly and over time. No one told us that they had always felt good about themselves right from the start. While it is certainly lamentable that we do not live in a world where all young people are raised to feel confident, worthy and grounded, this finding may also inspire hope. The way we feel about ourselves earlier in life is not set in stone but can be improved upon and developed over our lifespans. Openness and the willingness to learn from and embrace experiences may be crucial for this process. Extraordinary lovers were able to see difficult life events as opportunities for growth, learning, development and re-evaluation of previously-held ideas. Experiences such as illness, injury and/or disability often led to *improvements* in self-image and better sex for those who were not afraid to change themselves or their beliefs about sex and sexuality.

Maturity and Personal Development

Maturity was an important contributor to developing the capacity for magnificent sex and perhaps part of the reason that so many of our older participants told us that sex began to improve in their 50s, 60s or later. In this context, maturity was defined by a variety of processes, including supporting, validating, affirming, respecting and trusting oneself. Many people emphasized that maturity required an ongoing willingness to grow and change over time. (It should be noted that maturity was not predicated solely on chronological age but was also cited as important by younger individuals.)

Maturity helped extraordinary lovers be open to different kinds of experience: With a sense of being grounded and trust in oneself, risks and mistakes became less frightening and had less potential to be threatening. Being able to self-soothe and to tolerate anxiety and discomfort were considered valuable personal qualities and were sought after in partners. An older male participant emphasized the importance of trusting oneself:

> You have to be able to trust that whatever this is it's going to be the right thing, you know, it's going to work. Whatever it is, it's going to be the appropriate situation because if you start worrying about what's going to happen or 'Am I doing this right?' or 'Should I be doing this?' or 'Is it going to be okay?' then, you know, then you take your attention away from enjoying the flowering of the, of that sexual relationship.

One woman stated, "When you feel threatened, you can manage that inside yourself." Maturity is also related to the capacity to be present and centered in oneself.

Self-esteem and confidence are closely intertwined with conceptions of maturity. Extraordinary lovers describe themselves as being in charge of their own lives and responsible for the positive and negative consequences of their choices. A man stated that he was most attracted to older, mature women because "[they] know who they are." Or as a female sex therapist commented, "They can negotiate without feeling like they've sacrificed something."

Continued Growth Over Time

The journey towards magnificent sex was a long one for many people. They emphasized the need to continue growing, developing and maturing throughout their lives, both sexually and non-sexually. They described becoming more in tune with themselves over time and more authentic as they got older. One woman stated, "Because as you continue to get older, you're acquiring more experience, you're becoming a deeper, richer, more complex person. Your skills improve, your empathy improves, you can dance the dance a whole lot better."

Many said that their definitions of "great sex" and, indeed, of sex itself had changed and developed over time. For some, maturing involved a shift from a focus on the physical aspects of sex during their youth to a greater focus on the interpersonal qualities of the experience. Some specifically singled out the diminishing importance of orgasms as they got older. As one woman put it, "At this point, it's not so orgasm-oriented, it's more pleasure-oriented, which has ironically made the sex feel so much better [laughs]." Others said that the importance of the relationship in which sex occurred had grown over time. An older man recounted how his focus had shifted from having orgasms with gorgeous partners to, "Being with someone that you really want to be with."

Most emphasized that the pursuit of optimal sexual experiences could be an ongoing, lifelong journey and they were excited about the possibilities ahead of them. To put it another way, no one said that they had arrived at their destination, had accomplished everything on their list and had nothing more to learn about sex. In fact, some individuals described coming to new realizations and insights at every stage of their lives. Most said that they were still in the process of learning new things about themselves, their partners and sex itself even in their 60s and 70s. An older man explained:

> Well I wouldn't say I expect to be continually surprised 'cause I don't, but I do expect that there's more stuff I don't know. So [pause], I guess before any of them happened I was worried that I knew it all [laughs]. I'm very relieved to find out that there was more I had no idea of. And following, you know, each one that it, it becomes more the case that I realize sort of like the, my concept of the greatness of human experience and of my potential doesn't just double, it, you know, goes up by factors. So my experience is not only that I experience something more fabulous, more uh, expansive and energetic and engaging a larger horizon, but that I become aware that there are other horizons that that, you know, I'm, that I'm climbing a hill and every time I think I see a crest it's really just another one of these experiences where I come up over a crest which I thought was a crest and then it turns out the mountain is looming higher in front of me.

Extraordinary lovers acted as philosophers and scientists, questioning and studying their own lives. It was rare that people reacted with much surprise to our interview questions, which suggests that they had spent significant time reflecting on their own experiences so as to make sense of them. Not surprisingly, most of their responses were thoughtful and nuanced, and the memories they shared of optimal sexual experiences were strong and detailed. Many self-identified as lifelong students who were passionate about learning in many aspects of their lives.

Changing, Growing and Maturing Together

For magnificent sex to be possible long-term, it was important not only that extraordinary lovers embraced change and growth in themselves as individuals but that this attitude also characterized their relationships. Development and change over time was expected, embraced and encouraged by both partners. An older woman provided her equation for magnificent sex over the course of a lifetime: "Time coupled with . . . a growthful partnership, where people are learning and it's so multifaceted." An older woman expressed the belief that, "Sex becomes more genuine and more human" later in life.

Extraordinary lovers emphasize the need for fluidity and flexibility in their attitudes towards their partners, their relationships and sex itself, and expect that change will be continuing. They embrace growth in themselves and their partners through their emotional maturity, their openness to experience and their willingness to continue learning. One person felt that change was woven into her definition of "great sex":

> Great sex is changing sex, so maybe change is the difference between good sex and great sex. Great sex is when people change, their thoughts and emotions change and their physical connection with each other also changes. So that maybe great sex is where people are always learning new things about themselves and about each other about how to pleasure each other and they laugh and have a good time.

An older woman described the intersection between personal maturity and relational maturity:

> [Partners] can tolerate discomfort, even though they don't like it they can tolerate it. Change is inherent in the relationship . . . Each person can manage their own anxiety and share their growth with the other one . . . I don't know that we ever actually achieve maturity but, as long as we're trying, or as long as we're ahead in that way, I think a relationship can work.

The importance of accepting change and learning from it with a partner was emphasized by most of the older individuals, and especially by those who had been affected by illness or injury. This attitude was exemplified by an older woman: "Things may not work the way they always did so do you just shut it off and say 'I'm not going to do this anymore because it doesn't work the way it should' or do you say 'Okay, let's find another way to express our intimacy'?"

Knowledge, Depth and Shared History

In many cases, the accumulation of knowledge over time and deep familiarity at every level is part of what makes sex magnificent. This knowledge covers a wide spectrum, from the sexual to the non-sexual, including extraordinary lovers' bodies, their physical responses, their desires, feelings, thoughts, dreams and fears. They emphasized the importance of continually expanding and building on that knowledge throughout the duration of the relationship. A kinky man explained how knowledge was important with a music-inspired metaphor:

> It takes practice. You know, a great symphony, a great concert, has a conductor who knows what he's doing, has a score that's well-written, and has an orchestra that is professional and knows what they're doing. But when you put those three – and perhaps a great concert hall – but you put those four things together all at once and they don't know each other, it's going to take practice to produce that great symphonic concert.

Familiarity and the joy and pride people felt in their relationships could enhance the quality of sexual experiences. For some, part of what made sex utterly magnificent with a long-term partner was shared history together. People often related their favorite memories and reminisced about the important events in the relationship with us. They talked about the process of creating shared history, their awareness that they were working with their partners on a long-term project and the joy they took in what they were building together. An older man explained the importance of relationship history in both of his long-term partnerships:

> Every time that I'm with each one of them, part and parcel of what goes on during long, off-the-clock sex is historical discussion.

And reflection on who we are, what our history has been, where we've been, where we are, where we hope to be and, and with the acknowledgment that, um, there's an awesome dynamic in what's going on between and amongst the people involved.

The idea of familiarity and shared history also intersected with the idea of maturity and embracing change over time. People had been through so many ups and downs together, good times and bad, that they had developed a deep well of confidence and sense of stability. They knew at a bone-deep level that they could make it. An older woman explained why having a long history with her husband was important to her:

> My husband I have had, have known each other all these years and all of the history that we have with each other has added so many beautiful memories to our, to us . . . you build on it with good things and then the bad things can happen and there's still so much worth being around that other person that you're just glad you're able, being able to participate in no matter what's going on.

One older polyamorous woman explained why her best sexual experiences were still with her husband of 40-plus years:

> We have been through so much and through so many changes and have so much history . . . it makes a relationship that is just rich beyond measure . . . We have become like the spiral helix. We have constructed our mutual DNA with each other's.

Her husband, whom we interviewed separately, talked about the warmth of being in bed with someone for 40-plus years.

Compared to popular culture, which emphasizes important "firsts" and where virginity is prized, many of the extraordinary lovers said that sexual encounters were more likely to improve as their relationships progressed. One woman said:

> I was listening to a Sadé song the other day . . . and in this song it – that I totally disagree with – she says 'It's never as good as the first time.' And I certainly feel like the first time is usually not as good as it gets, as you get to *really* experience the other person, get to know each other, get to open up with each other, fine-tuning things. I mean [sighs] I think sex gets better with time, with a partner.

Newness and beginnings are fetishized in popular culture. Movies, music and books focus on first meetings, first kisses, first dates and first sexual encounters. The love story takes us from dating to marriage but not usually beyond the wedding. How many love stories take us 10 years into the marriage and show us the advantages of familiarity? Extraordinary lovers filled us in on the rewards of longevity and its contribution to magnificent sex. An older man compared and contrasted novelty and familiarity in his long-term marriage:

> Speaking as someone who's been in one relationship for, like forever, over 50 years, uh, there are certain things about the familiarity, the comfort, the security, the knowing what to ask for kind of things. That can make something that less exciting in terms of like, if you were measuring heart rate, the heart rate may not be as high. But the ultimate satisfaction and definition of it as a magnificent experience might be at least as equal to what it was when it was younger, when one was younger.

His wife, whom we interviewed separately, described (somewhat more poetically) her feelings when her husband strokes her: "Skin particularly changes after menopause, that's one of the downsides of getting older, or that I find a downside [laughing a little]. When he touches it, it feels to me like it was when it was young."

Extraordinary lovers describe the advantages of familiarity and trust that are only available in the context of a deeply intimate relationship. Magnificent sex is not an either/or proposition nor a zero-sum game. We need not sacrifice quality and excitement for comfort and familiarity. These elements can all grow and develop together, if we are inclined to work on them.

Continuing Developments: Transfer Across Relationships or Is There Life After Death?

Colleagues have asked us frequently whether these ways of being together are unique to the relationship or if they are translatable/transferable across relationships. The answer is unexpectedly both. Some of the individuals who responded to our recruitment blurbs were in their 70s and 80s. Among these were a few widows and widowers who wanted to know if they would qualify for participation in our research, having been in a marriage with magnificent sex for decades but having outlived their spouses. We were eager to interview them about their lives, past and present. They inevitably volunteered to answer the question that we dared not ask: Yes, there is optimal erotic intimacy after marriage and death. Having shared an experience so sublime with their lifetime partners meant that they carried within the knowledge of themselves, their own capacities for magnificent sex, the recognition that such experiences were possible, what they involved and what it took for them to have such experiences. That meant that they were able to have them with others, too (Kleinplatz, Ménard, Paradis et al., 2009).

It was not easy to find new partners but as they indicated, that was precisely the point: It was important not to settle. As one woman remarked: "If there's someone I really want to have that connection with then, then that happens but at this point in my life, I'm incredibly picky about who I engage myself with sexually." Several indicated that having experienced the heights of erotic intimacy, they could recognize the individuals who might make for new prospective matches for them and they were right. New partners were no substitute for their beloved late spouses. What they had shared was unique and irreplaceable (see Frankl, 1955). It did, however, give them the outlines of what to search for in new partners. We heard the same refrain from some of the more experienced individuals in consensually non-monogamous relationships. They, too, knew that they were capable of magnificent sex and therefore, were able to select others with whom to share new, unique, extraordinary erotic experiences.

5
PREPARATION

"How would you recognize great sex if you stumbled into it?" One older man laughingly replied: "I don't stumble into it, I plan it!" Intentional effort and thoughtful planning and preparation in the days and hours leading up to sexual encounters helps to make them wonderful for many people. It involves keeping sex and the relationship in mind, setting aside enough time, organizing around it and being specific.

Preparing the Environment

In planning for magnificent sex, extraordinary lovers talked about creating an environment for sex that would reflect their specific, personal preferences as well as their goals for that particular encounter. Participants emphasized that they could only describe their own preferred environment and not anyone else's. No one described a "one-size-fits-all" environment that would automatically lead to magnificent sex. Instead, they talked about being thoughtful and deliberate in their choices so as to create a situation that might be erotic, relaxing, comfortable or whatever they most desired for that moment.

That being said, there are some common threads in their answers. Most people emphasized the need to set up a private, safe space. In order to really let go and relax, extraordinary lovers needed to be sure that they would not be interrupted. Virtually all of the parents whom we interviewed highlighted the need to make appropriate child-care arrangements. As one older person stated, "I think [parents] like to be able to make noise without worrying about other people coming in. My grandmother used to say everybody needs to have Vaseline when they're having sex: You put it on the doorknob." They mentioned shutting off telephones, ignoring the doorbell and turning off electronic devices or "anything that blinks".

Comfort was a recurring theme that had become increasingly important for some over time due to pain or discomfort from injury or illness. They explained that the temperature of the room should be congruent with personal preference and that surfaces (e.g., the bed, table, carpet) should be supportive. One of the main goals in purposefully setting up the sexual environment is to minimize the experience of internal distractions that might take away from focusing on the moment. Setting up a comfortable and safe environment allows lovers to relax, focus and be fully present. One woman explained that the background of a sexual encounter should be non-intrusive, "to allow the experience to be foreground."

Many people told us that they intentionally kept their bedrooms tidy and well-stocked so that they would have everything they needed to enhance a sexual experience. They talked about having food and beverages readily available as well as condoms, lube, toys and anything else that they might want to have on hand. They spoke about creating a space where there was nothing to interfere or compete with the connection they built between themselves and their partners, where they could focus entirely on the experience. A kinky woman explained: "One thing that I've been recently doing is making sure our bedroom is always clean so that I'm not looking around and going, 'Oh fuck! I gotta to do laundry' . . . it's an oasis and it gets you into the moment." (Laundry was cited frequently as an example of a potential distraction.)

Aside from minimizing internal and external distractions, several individuals described setting up their bedrooms (or other preferred locations) so as to enhance sensuality and build eroticism. The need to engage multiple senses – sight, sound, smell, taste and touch – came up several times. An older woman said:

> When we're preparing for really special sex, for example, it's a lot of, um, setting the scene and making sure that it's going to engage the senses in as many ways as possible. And so, in our case, it's going shopping for, we tend to alternate kinds of, we always have something to drink and something to eat, not huge amounts of either, but, um, really careful thought about the taste and the spice and the fragrance of what's going to be consumed. And the fragrance, we have special fragrance that we reserve just for those times. And lighting a fire in the fireplace.

Many talked about purposefully heightening eroticism, but doing so in a deeply personal way. One woman explained, "And that degree of preparation, that scene setting, that, and because it's an alternate focus with us, it's so delicious to think about 'What am I going to do for him?'" A man explained why creating a sensual environment can enhance focus and improve the quality of sexual experiences:

> And the things that led to the great sex were things like a really fantastic fruit and cheese plate that everyone was just so sexually connected to their bodies because of the tastes and the smell, and you know, the candles that were around.

Other important details of the physical environment that were mentioned during interviews included lighting, music and mirrors, although each of these was subject to personal preference. "Flattering" lighting was often mentioned and far more people mentioned candles than fluorescents. When someone referred to the use of music, being music lovers ourselves, we always asked for more details. Many different types of music were mentioned, including classical music (especially Mozart), new-age, Celtic music, Native American music, drumming, bluegrass, Middle Eastern dance music, rap, heavy metal, Metallica, Pink Floyd and industrial music. A kinky woman, who had a preference for music with a good beat, explained, "It's easy to flog to."

It should be noted that a few people found our question about the environment absurd. "I think it's what you bring to the environment, it's not the environment itself," said one. To the question "What does it take for people to have great sex in the way of the environment?" one person replied in a bewildered tone of voice, "Enough room, I guess." For these lovers, the intensity of the connection that they experienced with their partners could make the environment entirely irrelevant. A few had had magnificent sex in seemingly uncomfortable situations (e.g., in a back alley, in the rain, while camping, on a ski hill) because of the passion and chemistry they felt with their partners. An older man explained why minimizing distractions might be irrelevant to the very best sexual experiences:

> The minimizing distractions is good but honestly if you're doing it right, you know, your concentration is on what you're doing and on your partner and what they're doing and, um, you can honestly put up with, uh, you know, there can honestly be quite a, quite a lot going on in the background and you don't really have to pay any attention to it at all.

Setting up the bedroom for sex is a favorite topic of sex manuals and lifestyle magazines. Extraordinary lovers set up their environments deliberately so as to facilitate those other important factors – being embodied and absorbed, feeling totally connected to a partner, luxuriating in eroticism – that help make a sexual experience magical.

We received an unexpected lesson on "preparation" and for that matter, on the meaning of "sex" in the course of asking how often they engaged in sex and what proportion of these events were "great". An older, diabetic man replied that as he was aging, his frequency of sexual activities decreased but that he and his wife devoted more time to each encounter and to ensuring that it was optimal:

> It used to be sex three times a week but now it's only once, but that one time is great. We're in our 70s and semi-retired so we don't generally have sex on the days we're working, Monday to Wednesday, and then we work only Thursday mornings. But when we get home from work on Thursday afternoons, that's when foreplay begins. We discovered years ago that we really don't like post-prandial sex. So on Thursday afternoons, we start foreplay in the kitchen. We cut up squares of proteins and carbs . . . you know, like bite-size pieces of cheese, prepared meats, chopped vegetables. We hate having to interrupt sex with having to cook and then clean up . . . it ruins the momentum. So this way, we never have to get out of bed when we're hungry except to run to the kitchen, have a few bites and then back to bed, except to go to the bathroom or shower. And we go on that way, having sex uninterrupted from Thursday afternoon until we have to go back to work on Monday morning. So we only have sex once a week now, but it lasts for 3½ days.

Setting Aside Enough Time

Another factor that was mentioned frequently in preparing for magnificent sex was setting aside sufficient time. As one of our participants explained, "You don't just drop into it." Although a few individuals described really great "quickies", most felt that they needed a few hours to connect with their partners, relax, get comfortable and really focus. An older man described his ideal environment for magnificent sex as, "a locked door and no need to look at a watch." In fact, some preferred to devote entire afternoons, days or even weekends to sex. They told us about intentionally setting aside a significant amount of time in order to bask in sexual sensations. An older man explained why he preferred to set aside lots of time in order to create optimal sexual experiences:

> You have to have enough time to put it off for a while, for a couple of hours to do all kinds of things beforehand is just fantastic. Whether it's bathing or showering or dancing or taking each other's clothes off and dancing together nude or whatever it is. So then when you finally get to the point of actually penetrating her, oh, it just is . . . That's where we were going with all of that, kind of the culmination of everything that led up to it. But on the other hand, everything that led up to it is equally as important as sexual intercourse.

While most of us seem perfectly able to understand why a five-course meal does not simply arrive fully-prepared on our dining room table in 30 minutes, many people still seem to expect that magnificent sex can be attained in less time than it takes a pizza to arrive. Given the number of factors that might play a role in getting to optimal sexual experiences, it stands to reason that setting aside sufficient time was identified as important by many of the people we interviewed. Although some readers might find this idea intimidating or overwhelming, recognizing that these experiences take time might be a liberating thought, one that enables more realistic expectations.

Preparing the Self

In addition to preparing their bedrooms (or kitchen or living room or dungeon), several people spoke about how they prepared their bodies for magnificent sex. Specifically, some thought that taking the time to groom themselves physically, which might include bathing, special clothing and attention to personal hygiene, contributed to the quality of their sexual experiences. Many cited personal cleanliness as an important prerequisite for optimal sexual experiences, a factor that helped to minimize distraction and enhance focus. For a few folks, special garments played a role in their best sexual encounters. An older woman described her preferred fabric:

> I mean the very best thing to do is to not get naked right away, but to dress in silk, because silk transmits body heat in such a tactile way, it's just really nice to be able to stroke somebody who's wearing silk.

A few others mentioned wearing or having their partners wear special under-wear or lingerie. One woman explained the thinking behind why she chooses to dress in particular ways for her partners:

> My husband is, he likes the Hanes cotton underwear look on women and my other significant other is a Victoria's Secret kind of guy. So putting on what I know they find attractive that also feels good to me, that's part of that preparation. It's part of that headspace of . . . creating sacred space, of setting aside the time and space that this is different . . . We're not going to take our baggage into the bed with us . . . This time is special, and we are both going to be, at this par-ticular time, the best person for each other that we possibly can be.

Notwithstanding the stereotype that every man loves sexy lingerie, this is a wonderful illustration of the context and more specific intention behind preparations.

For some, cultivation of optimal sexual experiences in their lives required ongoing care and attention to their bodies. A few stated that they deliberately kept themselves in good shape and sought out partners who were in good shape, believing that this was an outward sign that people respected themselves and their bodies. As an older man remarked, "What do I do [to have great sex]? I go to the gym three times a week. I try to keep fit. I eat well." One woman explained why keeping in shape was important:

> One of my lovers, it was very important that I went swimming. Because when we were together, we would fuck and my arms would kill me and we had a long-distance relationship and she would leave . . . I found that I really needed to continue swimming in order to maintain my shoulder muscles, which were really nec-essary to fuck her well when she came back again.

Preparing oneself is a great example of a behaviour with critical but indi-rect links to magnificent sex. It is not the case that brushing one's teeth or showering will lead directly and automatically to optimal sexual expe-riences, but they might be less likely to occur or they may not be as good without the preparation (it is difficult to be fully embodied and engaged in the moment if one is worried about spinach between the teeth or body odour).

Preparing the Relationship

In addition to preparing their bodies and their sexual spaces, participants also talked about "preparing" their relationships in the hours leading up to sex. As one person explained, "The sex is not what happens at the moment of the sexual encounter but often it's what's gone on before that." Another woman quoted a Hollywood legend in her answer:

> Brigitte Bardot said that great sex starts in the morning . . . I think what she meant by that is when you wake up, that you, that you kind of live out sexuality. That it's kind of in your mind, that it's part of the way you act with each other long before you're actually engaged in any kind of, you know, technical sex.

Extraordinary lovers talked about deliberately engaging with their partners to enhance feelings of warmth, closeness and connection in the hours before a sexual encounter. One woman explained, "The feeling leading into sex I think has to be kind of warm and close, and feeling connected and the sex being a way of furthering that expression." Almost everyone stressed that the mood going into sex should be positive; in fact, several went so far as to specify that they did not think "make-up sex" was likely to be great. They emphasized the importance of being able to let go and be vulnerable with their partners, which requires feeling good about one another or as one person put it, "being in a good space together." The preparatory contributors outlined in this chapter played a key role for the personal (Chapters 6 and 7) and relational contributors (Chapters 9 and 10) falling into place, like dominoes.

Extraordinary lovers endorsed a range of different activities for building good feelings with their partners. Many said that having a good conversation before sex could be helpful. As one woman remarked, "Talking is foreplay." Other recommendations included having dinner or drinks together, going to a concert, taking a drive into the countryside, hiking, giving one another massages, going to some type of event or even cleaning the house. One older woman recommended, "Any kind of activity that encourages people to focus on each other . . . anything that gets people to enjoy each other's company beforehand is likely to lead to good sex." Another older woman reported that working with her husband of 40+ years on a shared creative project had resulted in a sustained period of really magnificent sex. There were no cookie-cutter recommendations here about romance and building connection: True romance was defined at a very particular level by extraordinary lovers and their partners.

Even in good partnerships, it is usually not the case that every day or even every hour will be a perfect reflection of warmth and closeness that the relationship may (overall) embody. The need to assess the connection deliberately and purposefully and give it some attention so that the partners can be "in a good space together" going into a sexual encounter is incompatible with the stereotypical emphasis on "spontaneous" great sex. However, what is the purpose of dates in the early days of a relationship, if not to nurture and grow the bond, before "falling" into bed at the end of the night? Were those encounters truly spontaneous or did they not also involve a significant degree of preparation?

6

ENDURING
INDIVIDUAL QUALITIES

Individual qualities refer to those attributes, characteristics and/or skills that help to create magnificent sex. For virtually everyone we spoke with, the ability to create optimal sexual experiences had developed over their lives, and many believed that a combination of life experiences, their personal attributes and their choices had contributed to a steady improvement in the quality of their sexual experiences over time. Many people also said that certain qualities had become more or less salient over time: Some elements became less important, others became more important and, in some instances, new qualities were discovered, either within themselves or in their partners. In this chapter, we do not divide the list into "my own personal qualities that facilitate magnificent sex" and "the qualities of my partners that facilitate magnificent sex" because the participants themselves did not take this approach. The qualities that most believed were necessary in themselves were also seen as necessary from their partners. It should also be emphasized that no one expected all of these qualities to be present all of the time in any one person and some individuals emphasized certain qualities over others.

Glass Half-Full, Sex-Positive People

Many people reported that their *non-sexual* attitudes and values towards life were important contributors to magnificent sex. Their personalities outside of the bedroom carried over into sex, and they described themselves as optimistic, enthusiastic, "glass half-full" types with a zest for life. They were passionate and enthusiastic and inclined to focus on the positive with other kinds of life experiences – and they were also passionate and enthusiastic about and inclined to see the positive about sex. This was borne out by their enthusiastic answers to interview questions and in the laughter that permeated the interview recordings (and sometimes made the transcription process challenging). An older man described his life philosophy:

> When I was in physics, we learned about entropy and everyone else was like, 'You know, we should really be depressed about this because the universe is running down and there's nothing we can do about it' and I'm like, 'No, that's what life is really like.' That's why we're here, 'cause if we weren't here, there wouldn't be this universe. But we wake up every morning and we put in the positive energy that rewinds the clock and keeps things going and moves the universe forward. And it's sort of like the half-full, half-empty thing except it's really not about that but the glass. It's like about if you look at a glass, do you see the smudges on the glass, do you have judgments about what's in the glass? Or do you just enjoy the fact that a blade of light comes through the glass, and the fact that there's something in it which you can then take into your body and it will create more life in yourself which you can then multiply many-fold and put that back into. So, I think that it really is just keeping your intentions pure, keeping your sense of proportion so that you don't really get distracted from the power of the creative spirit by all this entropy that's going on around you all the time.

Adopting an attitude of joyful enthusiasm towards life itself and towards sex enhanced both.

Although it may seem an obvious contributor to magnificent sex, many people made a point of saying that they enjoyed sex. A male sex therapist was asked what might lead people to have great sex. He replied:

> I would imagine that they just . . . [laughing] This is going to sound real deep: They just like it. I think people who have great sex on some level just have a guilt-free kind of, just comfort with saying that they just like sex.

One man said: "I think being positive about it is a good thing and I enjoy it and I don't make any secret about it." They unabashedly delighted in sex, in themselves and in their partners as sexual beings. It was also clear that extraordinary lovers saw themselves as sexual beings and that their sexuality was inseparable from the rest of themselves. As one older woman said, "I believe how one feels about their sexuality permeates through every bit of their life." Sex and sexuality were not compartmentalized but were well-integrated aspects of their personalities. As a result perhaps of this integration between the sexual and non-sexual sides of self, the pursuit of optimal sexual experiences was not treated as substantially different from the pursuit of excellence in other areas (e.g., work, hobbies, relationships).

This finding may seem obvious. However, it can be considered a radical stance in a society where it is often unacceptable to acknowledge the pursuit of sexual pleasure or to claim enjoyment of certain types of sexual activities. Women are often "slut-shamed" for having numerous partners; men are mocked for focusing on quality over quantity. However, owning an interest in sex and not feeling shame over it may be an essential prerequisite to devoting the time and energy to cultivate these experiences.

Wanting Magnificent Sex

Going beyond simply self-defining as "sex positive" as a static personal quality, one of the most basic contributors to having optimal sexual experiences was really wanting to have them and then putting in the time, energy and effort to make them happen. As one woman explained:

> You have to know that good sex doesn't just fall out of the sky, that it has to be a priority because otherwise the trash has to be taken out and the meals have to be planned and tomorrow's chores have to be planned . . . and *Grey's Anatomy* is going to be on in 20 minutes and there's always something else that has to be tended to. If sex isn't seen as important, it'll quit being that way and I think that's really a very easy way for sex to become lackluster. And I think many, many people just wait for it, wait for the stars to fall from the sky rather than plucking them from the sky and, and bringing 'em home.

This may be one of the more important beliefs to "unlearn" – that magnificent sex is not a magical experience that works unpredictably, like a Vegas slot machine. Rather, these encounters require a high level of interest and intent and – like most other activities in life – require commitment in order to see improvement.

Extraordinary lovers did not hesitate to dedicate significant effort and commitment to the pursuit of optimal sexual experiences, as well as to learning more about themselves, their partners and sex. A woman described a relationship that involved lots of magnificent sex:

> One lover of mine, we used to get together on Friday night . . . and then spend all day Saturday together and all day Sunday together and we would part Monday morning . . . we didn't make plans with ten people and we didn't make plans to do ten things and we got together on Friday night, we both had the time available and, and that swallowed up the whole weekend . . .

A choice may be necessary. Magnificent sexual experiences may require a conscious decision to pursue, develop and cultivate them. People may need to consider whether this is something they wish to pursue in earnest and are prepared to devote the necessary time and energy to bring it about. One man stated:

> I think there has to be some sort of . . . dedication to it. Some sort of, you know, thought. For me, I think it's the feeling . . . for people that are religious, that go to church, it's an ongoing thing, you know, that you do every day. You don't necessarily have sex every day but you sort of think about it every day and you think about the possibilities and you think about the different people that you might have sex with and you pursue it, in a way.

Another woman echoed this statement when asked about the characteristics of people who have magnificent sex:

> One of the characteristics is they've got to want it. Like I don't think great sex happens to people who *don't* want sex. But if you want it, you don't have to have hands, you don't have to have genitals. You have to have some part of your body that's organized so that it can provide some form of satisfaction.

Enjoying sex and self-defining as a sex-positive person may not be enough. Bringing magnificent sex into one's life may require a decision to be made, and possibly some sacrifices as well. It may not be possible to excel at work, keep the house spotless, train for a marathon, read to the children every night and pursue magnificent sex all at the same time. Although this could seem like a disheartening statement, in fact, our intention is to be liberating. If sex is not amazing and wonderful and mind-blowing right now, it may simply be that it is not a priority at this point in life and cannot be because other areas of life need more attention. Magnificent sexual experiences do require wanting them to happen and committing substantial time and energy but, as our older participants demonstrated so beautifully, they will be available down the road when other life commitments ease up.

Actively Seeking Out Magnificent Sex

Once extraordinary lovers made the decision that optimal sexual experiences were important and worth pursuing, they then actively sought out different life experiences in order to build their capacities and skills. One older man described his journey:

> I had an enormous range of opportunities and capitalized on them. Was able to explore all aspects of my fantasies and desires to great lengths. And through that process became increasingly skilled and learned about what, what I wanted and how to get it.

They looked for opportunities to learn more about sex and about themselves. Some read books, others attended formal workshops or took classes and some joined special-interest communities (e.g., polyamory, kink). As one man described his learning and experimentation: "Let's try something outside the box. Let's not do the safe stuff that Mommy said was okay. Let's get on the Internet, see what's out there." They sought out information in order to develop their knowledge and skills, both in sexual and non-sexual ways. A few told us about books that changed in their lives, including *Sex for One* by Betty Dodson and *The Inner Game of Golf* by Timothy Gallwey. (The golfing manual was mentioned by so many of the people we interviewed that we both read it. They were correct – it is relevant for sex, too. Great sexual experiences, like great golf games, require intense focus on the present and the ability to let go of self-criticism and judgment. However, neither the quality of sexual experiences nor of golf games is determined solely by the functioning of the relevant body parts – for example, arms, in the case of golf and tennis, or genitals, with regard to sex.)

Extraordinary lovers talked about learning from partners and learning with partners, taking recommendations from friends or play partners. Quite a few people focused on improving their skills in non-sexual areas, such as acquiring better communication and negotiation skills or developing massage techniques. Several described the BDSM community as an excellent resource for information and learning on sexual communication.

Regardless of their participation in formal learning opportunities, most were enthusiastic proponents of the "trial-and-error" approach. As one man explained:

> It's just been a process of trying different things, hearing about something and enjoying at least how it sounded, and then trying it to see if I like how it feels. And then finding people who are willing to do those things with me.

Another man described his learning process:

> I see it almost like painting a painting. That sometimes you can paint a painting that, at the end of it, you feel it's not successful but the very fact of it not being successful is what sort of moves you on, drives you on to create another. So there's always this element of search, of wanting to find, whether it's to find the right partner or to find the right intensity or to find a connection in some sense, a deep, deep, deep connection.

Engaging in these activities was important, but it was the intent and the follow-through that mattered more than the activities themselves. Many people report engaging in the same activities as these participants (e.g., having sex with many partners, practising new techniques, reading books on the subject) but do not reap the same benefits. In fact, some of them may be more miserable than when they started. The difference may be in the intent and the purpose, which lead to very different outcomes. The point of these learning activities was not to focus on mechanics, techniques and "guaranteed" strategies. The point, for our participants, was to learn more about themselves and their partners and to explore new sexual territory. It is deliberate reflection and self-awareness that makes the difference. As one woman explained:

> You can have two partners over the course of your life and as long as you're willing to sexually evolve with them and the communication evolves proportionately, and an adventuring spirit and a willingness to try what does and does not work accompanies those two partners or 200 partners, I think that's the key.

Curiosity, combined with motivation, dedication, commitment and reflection seemed to be a crucial combination in the quest for optimal sexual experiences. Having identified the types of sexual experiences or partners that were most relevant to them, extraordinary lovers developed their capacities for optimal sexual experiences through practice, repetition and refinement.

Being Ready and Willing

In 2011, as our research team was studying transcripts, Meghan Campbell, Psy.D., observed that if there were one core element that the individual brings to the enterprise of magnificent sex, it was the sheer willingness to go there. "You know," she said, "As in the show *Being Erica* on CBC" [i.e., the Canadian Broadcasting Corporation]. Dr. Campbell was correct and so was her analogy to *Being Erica*. The protagonists on this program are Erica and a character named "the Therapist". At the outset of each episode, the Therapist shows Erica a corridor with a series of doors, each opening to a pivotal moment in her past. The Therapist offers Erica the opportunity to go back in time to have a do-over, to see what other paths her life might have taken had she chosen differently. The moment is fraught with possibilities – all irrelevant unless Erica is willing to let go and enter the adventure. This, Dr. Campbell suggested, is the essential attitude required to enable sex to become extraordinary: willingness. Is that sufficient? Surely not. It is an eternal theme in literature and on film, from the *Bible* to the *Odyssey* to *Alice in Wonderland*, the *Phantom Tollbooth* and the *Matrix*. Without that inclination to open doors to new experience, all else is impossible.

The journey towards optimal sexual experiences involved two parallel but complementary processes. Some learning was achieved through active pursuit, by deliberately seeking, choosing and pursuing specific experiences, whether sexual or not. Other learning came through receptive openness – being ready, willing and able to learn from opportunities when they appeared, sometimes spontaneously. One process was planned and self-determined, the other process was unplanned and unpredictable. Essentially, the distinction is akin to ordering something unusual or different off a restaurant menu, knowing what dish you will receive, versus ordering the "chef's surprise", which could be anything at all. Both approaches were important and useful.

Being open to and embracing the possibilities for learning required courage, fearlessness, mental flexibility and the ability to stay grounded. Extraordinary lovers welcomed the unexpected into their lives and their bedrooms, "being open to the spontaneous", as one woman put it. Although these opportunities could not be predicted or planned, the people we spoke with talked about cultivating a non-judgmental openness to new learning opportunities so that they would be available when necessary. One woman explained:

I certainly kept my eyes open, listened, heard other people and, and what made their sex feel wonderful to them, experimented with myself and my own body, you know, sort of was open to whatever media influences were out there that seemed like, 'Hmm, this is an interesting direction to go' or 'This could make things feel kind of great.'

One man said:

I've always been really interested to try almost anything that can be done safely. Um, you know, figuring the worst thing that happens is I don't like it, but I've tried lots of different foods that I didn't think I was gonna like until I actually ate them, so, I've always brought that attitude to sex, too.

(Foodies and people who want to improve their sex lives may have much to learn from one another.) The pursuit of magnificent sex may require being open to possibilities, trying new things, taking risks and learning from the experience. As an older woman commented, "There's always more to learn, if you're open to it." Or as one sex therapist observed, "I think experience teaches a lot *for people who want to learn*."

Extraordinary lovers talked about the need to be open, free, daring, curious and open-minded. One man described his ideal partner as, "Willing to do things that she had always imagined her mother would roll over in her grave if she did that." Just as non-sexual optimism carried over into the bedroom, being ready and willing also crossed over from the sexual to the non-sexual domains for some individuals and their partners. Another man described his favorite partners:

They were willing to learn and to go to another depth of participation. I saw them as people who were here to grow, and that also carried into a lot of other things about their lives. 'Here, I've shown you this and now let me show you this, this and this. Have you ever heard flamenco music? Let's go hear it [starts laughing]. Have you ever done this? Let's go do it!'

People emphasized the need to pay attention to their environment, their partners and their sexual encounters in order to identify chances for learning and expansion. One man said, "I feel you learn something from every sexual encounter that you have, from every person that you're with, it's a teachable moment if *you choose to pay attention to it*." Instead of avoiding situations that had the potential to cause embarrassment, fear or anxiety, these feelings were embraced with openness and curiosity. Although their adventures did not always meet with success, they used these experiences to refine their knowledge and skills. A woman laughed off her not-so-successful experiences: "When you experiment as much as I do, you're going to go down some [laughing] dead ends, do you know what I mean?" Another woman stated:

> And if I had to say that I was taught great sex by anyone, I'd have to say everyone I've ever had. Even the worst lays in history taught me about good sex . . . If nothing else, they're good for a bad example [laughter]. 'Oh look, that's not great sex.' You know, I don't think I'll do that again. Process of elimination, trial and error.

Failures or less-than-perfect encounters were processed and let go without feelings of shame or guilt.

The beauty of adopting an attitude of openness and willingness is that if one wishes to improve the quality of one's sexual experiences, the world then becomes an endless series of learning opportunities. Every partner, every sexual encounter, even hobbies like golf or tennis have the potential to provide valuable insights that may be applied to sex and sexuality. It is the intention, the awareness and the approach that can make all the difference. The pursuit of optimal sexual experiences may simply require an adjustment in mindset.

Self-Awareness

Extraordinary lovers emphasize the importance of self-awareness in reference to both the sexual and non-sexual areas of their lives. The creation of optimal sexual experiences required an ongoing access and adjustment to their inner worlds. They devoted time to processing their own thoughts, emotions and reactions so that they could remain attuned to their authentic selves. Again, there is an important element here related to tolerating discomfort in the service of growth as this type of reflection is not always easy. The result of this reflective process was, for some, a mental and spiritual grounding and an enhanced ability to be fully present in their lives.

In some cases, individuals told us about a pivotal moment, a decision made to live more authentically. For some, this meant accepting and living out specific desires and sexual interests such as embracing polyamory or BDSM. For others, this meant embracing their sexual orientations or gender identities. For others, it was just the realization that their existing blueprints for sex were inadequate or unrewarding. Across the board, the commonality is that they recognized that something was not working, that it needed to change, and that they were willing to take steps in a new direction. This event often had a domino effect on the quality of their sexual experiences. An older gay man described his journey to magnificent sex:

> Well, it took me a while to figure out about relationships. Being gay in the early sixties wasn't – I never knew any people I knew were gay and I didn't even know it was a possibility until it happened the first time. And then the common wisdom seemed to be that it was always accidental, furtive, and . . . it had nothing to do with any kind of ongoing relationship or deepening of feelings. And so, when I discovered that actually you could have a relationship with someone that also included great sex, that made . . . great sex a lot more exciting.

Magnificent sex may require understanding, awareness and, most of all, acceptance of desires, preferences and interests. Extraordinary lovers emphasized again and again that optimal sexual experiences must come from within and that their understanding of themselves must be updated and improved over time. One woman explained:

> I think that you need to allow yourself the freedom to grow sexually as you allow yourself to grow in any other way in your life. I have a friend who prefers to describe her sexual appetites as meat and potatoes and she describes mine as the smorgasbord [laughter]. And she is not prepared to be a part of the smorgasbord. She's just looking for meat and potatoes.

One man thought that this improved knowledge of self had resulted in greater and greater sex over time:

> I would say that the, the older I got, the higher proportion of greatness because, um, [pause] I learned what I will compromise and won't compromise, I learned more what behaviours are more erotic to me than others and I've had a, um, developed a very good ability in being able to find partners who are interested in those eroticisms and how to bring it out with them.

Self-awareness is often an early step on the road to cultivating magnificent sex. From developing a better understanding of oneself, continually refining this knowledge and being willing to move forward, it becomes possible to make better choices in terms of experiences and partners. For some, this may be a radical decision and change, but for others, it may be a series of smaller refinements. Either way, the take-home message should be that optimal sexual experiences are deeply personal and individual and require high levels of honesty, which certainly may be challenging and perhaps uncomfortable. However, we argue that not acknowledging one's true desires and enduring unrewarding sex is also uncomfortable and, unlike the journey towards greater authenticity, is unlikely to be associated with long-term growth.

The Laundry List

Sometimes, in addition to the qualities and attributes listed above, individuals would offer examples of their particular preferences for sexual partners. In many cases, their descriptions resembled a personal ad or "laundry list". Often, they would spontaneously remark that not all of these qualities were absolutely essential, or that they were less important than other characteristics or even that all of these traits were unlikely to exist in any one person. But they wanted to share their lists of preferences and ideals.

Creativity, a sense of humour and imagination were qualities that were considered highly desirable in a partner. One man said that he particularly enjoyed being able to see someone's "inner child", and felt that such a person would have a greater capacity for playfulness and spontaneity. Generosity, kindness, compassion and patience were often mentioned. Intelligence was cited by a few people, although they were usually quick to point out that they did not equate this with high educational achievement or IQ. One woman explained, "I think there are a wide variety of intelligences. I personally prefer someone who's well-read, who has some sort of a background in film and art, especially as it relates to popular culture." Or as one man put it, "They gotta be someone that you can have a decent conversation with."

A few people mentioned specific physical qualities (e.g., height, weight, colouring) that they were looking for or preferred in sexual partners. However, these same people were also likely to emphasize that their partners need *not* be considered conventionally attractive. A few individuals specifically mentioned that they preferred "unconventional" folks, whether this referred to their partners' personal appearance, career or hobbies. One man described his preferred partners: "They're kind of interesting in that they've approached life and, and really done it in some unique way that makes me sort of admire them and find them interesting."

7
INDIVIDUAL QUALITIES IN-THE-MOMENT

If the previous chapter was focused on the enduring personal characteristics which contributed to magnificent sex, this chapter will focus on how these and other characteristics play out during the course of an optimal sexual experience. For example, those who generally have the capacity to focus, center themselves and ignore distractions might find these qualities particularly useful to draw upon while in the midst of sex. People who are optimistic and enthusiastic most of the time may find their sexual experiences better if they are able to bring this forth in the moment. In fact, most of the contributors described in this chapter do seem to be linked to the attributes, qualities or skills discussed in Chapter 6. The focus of this chapter is on the individual factors that contribute to making sex magnificent *while it is happening*. These include managing expectations, feeling enthusiasm, being totally embodied, absorbed and focused, going beyond oneself and being ready, willing and open.

Managing Expectations

Extraordinary lovers offered contradictory thoughts on the role of expectations related to optimal sexual experiences. Some said that it was important not to have any expectations going into sexual encounters. They recommended letting go of "shoulds" and "musts", dropping preconceived ideas about themselves, their partners or sex itself, and going into it in the spirit of openness and curiosity. One man explained:

If I go into it saying, 'This is going to be great sex,' you know, oftentimes that just makes it not happen. If I go into it with the attitude of, 'Well, you know, let's have fun and let's see what happens and make sure that everybody's enjoying themselves', then it's a lot more likely.

Another person said, "I don't put expectations around sex. I don't expect it to be great, I don't expect it to *not* be great, I just expect it to be." Some talked about aiming for sex that was fun, pleasurable, connected, relaxed or satisfying rather than exceptional. Extraordinary lovers made a particular effort not to let their own outdated and potentially toxic ideas intrude on sex as it was happening. As one man explained: "When you think that that good sex has to do with paying attention to your own movie and making reality agree with a movie, that, that's a big obstacle to having it work for me now."

However, others felt that their positive expectations about sex helped to improve it, that their hopes going into a sexual encounter might actually contribute to bringing about magnificent sex. They described a positive feedback loop whereby their positive expectations helped draw their attention to the positive, to immerse themselves in the experience and be more present. For example, when asked "What do you do to have great sex?" one older woman answered:

Think [laughing], I think myself into trouble! . . . I always seem to be very much of an optimist and I always think the glass is half-full and I always think I'm going to have a wonderful time. And sometimes I do and sometimes I don't, but more often than not, I think I do, because I am telling myself that I'm going to.

One man said that realizing in the moment that a particular sexual encounter was "destined for greatness" could actually help make that happen.

Perhaps one of the more important aspects of having expectations is to share them with a partner. Some felt that it was helpful to clarify the purpose of the encounter with their partners, to ensure that they were on the same page. On some occasions, the shared goal was to try to create an optimal sexual experience; on other occasions, it might be simply to experience pleasure together, build or rebuild connection or just to get off. One person explained how to set up appropriate goals for a sexual encounter with his partners:

If you aim for perfect, you're never gonna reach it. But if you aim for good enough, sometimes you actually do reach perfect. And so what I aim for is, you know, good enough in that sense of, 'Is everybody enjoying themselves? Are they feeling good? Are they taken care of? Is their health, pleasure, consent and wellbeing all supported? Then great!' And some of the time that leads to a more transcendent, great sex kind of place and sometimes it doesn't. I don't try to force it.

Clarifying and managing expectations was related to "unlearning" and "letting go" of outdated scripts and/or inaccurate and harmful myths about sexuality. This was true both in extraordinary lovers' overall, day-to-day lives as well as during sexual encounters. The decision to let go of a negative message or a harmful belief is not a one-time occurrence but rather is an ongoing commitment that must be renewed as needed, which may include before, during and after sex. Some people find their experiences, not just sexually but overall, are enhanced when they expect good things to come their way because it leads them to focus on the positive and become more open to the possibilities around them. It may also be the case that certain expectations are more helpful and "workable" than others. The key is to develop greater awareness around which thoughts are useful and which are not.

Feeling Enthusiasm

Extraordinary lovers described themselves as optimistic and sex-positive, and they were not afraid to let these qualities shine through during sexual encounters. They said that during sexual encounters, they would dive in, have fun, experience joy and feel playful. They talked about being enthusiastic, eager and passionate about their partners and sex itself. One man felt that magnificent sex involved "just being totally high on being with a person." One woman was describing her favorite partners:

> The ones that it's the best are the ones that are kind of like me in terms of being able to be lost in the moment, to go with the flow, to scream if they're having sex and, you know, revel in it.

Another man talked about how much he appreciated his partner's "animalistic reactions" and "absolute, uncontrollable wild abandon." Extraordinary lovers talked about feeling inspired, creative and energetic during the experience.

Those who were optimistic and enthusiastic about the role of sex in their lives were able to draw on this energy during sexual experiences and share it with the right partners. Feeling "happy to be there", as one woman put it, may be related to being fully absorbed on all levels. Feeling free to be themselves and being completely immersed in the moment enhanced feelings of happiness and enthusiasm. Once they were in a position to create magnificent sexual experiences, extraordinary lovers expressed their joy openly and enthusiastically. These were people who unabashedly and unapologetically loved sex and were not afraid to let it all out in the moment. Showing enthusiasm was facilitated over time by those who had found greater comfort in their own bodies, working gradually towards lower levels of self-consciousness (Chapter 6).

Being Utterly Absorbed, Embodied and Focused

Almost everyone we interviewed said that feeling completely absorbed during a sexual encounter was important; in fact, this was often identified as one of the most important factors in helping to make a sexual experience magnificent. Extraordinary lovers reported that optimal sexual experiences required them to be completely focused, committed and present in the moment. This level of embodiment involves both tuning in to the experience and tuning out internal and external distractions. People needed to focus on the sexual encounter at hand and let go of worries about work, parenting or household chores, at least temporarily. "Shutting down the part of my head that gets in the way", as one man put it. Another person said: "You just have to be in the experience more than you have to be about controlling or understanding it or managing it or taking a critical point of view towards it." Several described this mental stance as "being available".

Extraordinary lovers also talked about how important it was to feel deeply connected to their bodies during magnificent sex and they used words such as "savouring", "luxuriating", "basking" and "revelling" in order to capture this experience. As one woman said, "The greatest are when they're, I'm *really* in my own, you know, very present in my body with my feelings rather than thinking." As another woman said, "I really can dive into my own body." They described tuning in to their inner worlds and immersing themselves in sensation and pleasure. There was a reciprocal and reinforcing relationship between being physically and mentally present. Being completely present on a physical level and tuning in to the sensations helped lovers to focus on the sexual experience. Likewise, allowing sexual experience to completely occupy their entire awareness helped them to feel grounded in their bodies.

People who, in general, had good centering skills (see Chapter 8) could draw on them in the course of a sexual experience. Their ability to focus helped to enhance the quality of the sex and their experience of immersion was part of what made the sex magnificent. Developing the ability to focus at a high level might be a challenge to master but it may become easier as the sex itself becomes more compelling. It may also be the case that being able to focus and be present during sex enhances one's ability to be focused and present in non-sexual realms and, correspondingly, that practice of these skills both inside and outside the bedroom may pay off in all domains. Being able to center and ground oneself, both in everyday life and during sex, may be linked with developing a sense of comfort in one's body. People who spent time fully inhabiting their bodies felt relaxed and comfortable with themselves, both during sex and in general. In many cases, the experience of wonderful sex may have a significant impact on developing greater comfort with one's self.

Going Beyond Oneself

Many talked about how going beyond themselves could help make a sexual experience magnificent. What did they mean by this? Extraordinary lovers told us that during magnificent sex, they were able to experience something bigger, broader or deeper, something transcendent or transformative, something beyond the mundane. One older man said that for him, magnificent sex required a connection to "the creative heart of the world or . . . the life force". Another person said: "I would say that the truly great ones really take me and the person I'm with, take me to another realm. And it really takes me almost out of my body even as I'm very much in it."

Generally, those who described going beyond themselves during optimal sexual experiences did not say that this was a regular feature of their non-sexual lives. That is, being able to go beyond oneself during magnificent sex did not seem to require being formally religious in one's everyday life. However, it may require the ability to be open and willing to embrace the unexpected.

Being Ready, Willing and Open

Just as being open to learning from any person and any situation may lead to learning experiences in general, so too may openness in the course of a sexual experience lead to the learning and growth that are conducive to experiencing magnificent sex.

The willingness to be emotionally available and vulnerable during sex was crucial in creating optimal erotic intimacy. It was important to be flexible, try new things and be willing to make mistakes. One man described his experience of freedom and being able to let go:

> The total freedom to do anything and everything and the feeling that that other person with you feels the same way – or those other people with you feel the same way – so that in the moment, something you didn't even think about might just occur.

Being open on a personal level was associated with a capacity for spontaneity and a loss of inhibitions. As one man described it, "No holds barred." Another person described this feeling as, "Whatever in the moment feels right and your body seems to enjoy and your partner seems to enjoy." Many told us that magnificent sex required a person to let go, to give in and go with the flow. A woman explained how she recognized optimal sexual experiences: "I would feel comfortable pushing myself in my boundaries, um, and asking for something new perhaps or . . . um offering something that normally I wouldn't offer to someone." Another woman said:

> There is a confidence of being able to be open to the moment of, um, being able to say, 'You know what? I'm going to go into this with the plan that we're going to do X, Y, and Z but I'm not going to worry about it if when I do X, I end up going into L and M instead.' I'm just going to know that whatever happens is exactly what's supposed to happen. If I find myself doing things that are totally out of character for me, I'm not going to freak out, I'm just going to go with it [laughing].

Instead of avoiding situations that might cause fear and anxiety, extraordinary lovers embraced these feelings with openness and curiosity. Although their adventures did not always meet with success, such individuals used these as learning experiences. Maintaining an attitude of welcoming openness to opportunities was important at all times but was particularly useful during sexual encounters. Sex presented unique opportunities for surprises and learning, especially if a participant was deliberately setting out to explore with a partner.

Learning to be open during a sexual encounter may be unnerving or uncomfortable, if not downright scary, and is certainly not a quality that we often value or encourage. Being out of control is generally seen as a bad thing and not something that we teach children (or adults!) to feel comfortably. Developing this quality in non-sexual situations may be a prelude to being able to draw on it during sexual encounters.

8
SKILLS

We now introduce the skills involved in or even required in magnificent sex. As astute readers may have gleaned by now, this will be a short chapter. Extraordinary lovers tended to raise an eyebrow when asked about skills, essentially letting us know, again, that we asked some odd questions – as though sexual "skills" were particularly relevant for erotic intimacy. Nonetheless, what they viewed as the few skills important for optimal sexual experiences was illuminating. These were centering abilities, fundamental knowledge of techniques and anatomy, knowledge and skills specific to the partner(s) in the encounter and empathic communication skills.

Centering Abilities

The ability to center oneself so as to completely and totally inhabit the present moment was one of the most relevant skills to creating optimal sexual experiences. The capacity to focus and be embodied was relevant across multiple areas, including mentally, physically, spiritually and emotionally. Extraordinary lovers described cultivating an intense focus on themselves and their partners that required blocking off or deliberately shutting down both internal and external distractions. An older man who was asked "What do you do to have great sex?" responded:

> My mind immediately goes to St. John on the Cross, you know, he converted, saw visions . . . he was talking about basically having sex, seeing God like that, and his key to it was purifying the soul. That is, training yourself to not be distracted by stuff like the daily news, you know, advertisements and the fact that the dishes are dirty.

One woman described the ongoing struggle to be present:

> It's the presence that's really the important thing, and that is
> something that I think I've known ever since the beginning. But
> over years, you kind of forget it as you get really busy with your
> life and it has to be brought back to you again, it seems like over
> and over again. Because it's a lesson that you keep learning – at
> least, I keep learning myself.

This comment is important not only because it is a good illustration of an
important sexual skill but also because it shows that it was generally not the
case that anyone had an amazing, God-given ability to create perfect, fantastic
sexual encounters at every opportunity. Even once it is clear what makes sex
magnificent and what helps make that happen, optimal sexual experiences
may still require ongoing effort and investment of time and energy.

Learning how to become centred and focused in non-sexual areas may be
good practice for developing the capacity to do so during sex. One man told
us how he had learned to concentrate during sex (which we do NOT recom-
mend for obvious reasons):

> It's matter of intense concentration that I hesitate to call it a
> Zen-like state because I don't really know that much about Zen.
> But it's certainly a state of mind, it's something that I personally
> learned how to do by riding motorcycles excessively fast on public
> roads. The way I described it is essentially if I am doing that, my
> world shrinks down until there is nothing in it except the piece of
> road between my front wheel and the next curve and the sound
> of the engine and the feel of the bike and the bars and the feet
> on footbrakes and that's all there is in my world at that point is
> the concentration works like that. And having learned to do it on
> motorcycles, it transferred over into sex and kink very easily.

Conversely, for some, the experience of being completely and fully present
during sex allowed them to feel more grounded and centered in their everyday lives.

A word of clarification here: Being present in this context is quite a bit
different from the extremely-popular mindfulness movement that has taken
off in the last two decades (e.g., Farb, 2014; van Dam et al., 2018). Mindfulness is usually defined of late as a non-judgmental awareness of the present,
a kind of detached observation of the contents of consciousness. If one is

being mindful, one can label thoughts and emotions as thoughts and emotions without being consumed by them, which can be very helpful in managing difficult internal experiences. However, being present, embodied and focused in this context sounded more like being consumed by the experience, completely fused with it to the point of abandoning self-consciousness. Both mindfulness and being present involve being in touch with the moment as it unfolds, but the former requires detachment while the latter requires total immersion. This is not to say that improving one's mindfulness skills might not be relevant for magnificent sex as far as being aware of and managing distractions. However, developing the capacity for this type of immersion and loss of self might be an entirely different skill, one that requires its own specific training and practice.

The ability to focus so deeply as to lose the self and be entirely immersed in a sexual encounter may be one of the most critical skills to develop, both as an individual and alongside a partner. Although there is occasional lip service from books, magazines and websites to the idea that sex is "between the ears", most advice still tends to focus on genital manipulation skills rather than mental skills, as though specific techniques can be expected to override a distracted mind. This finding is also another example of the integration between the sexual and the non-sexual, and speaks to the need to see sex holistically rather than separate it from other valued activities. People who learned to focus by riding motorcycles, playing an instrument or meditating applied these skills, with wondrous results, in the bedroom. The converse may also be true: Those who learn to focus and immerse themselves in the bedroom may be able to apply these skills in other important life domains and reap benefits there as well.

Sexual Knowledge and Skills

Just as pop culture sources tend to focus on the necessity of specific sex acts (e.g., oral sex, intercourse), there is also a strong emphasis on technique. Self-help books instruct that readers master important skills in the area of stimulation techniques, sensual touching, sex games and special positions in order to bring their partners to heights of pleasure.

Although most people de-emphasized the contribution of "techniques" to magnificent sex, quite a few said that having a basic level of knowledge and skills related to sex could be useful. In this context, skills are not thought of as a "one-size-fits-all great sex button", as one person characterized the typical *Cosmopolitan* philosophy. Rather, having a good knowledge of techniques provided a base on which to build and allowed for the creativity, confidence and flexibility that were necessary to create deeply personal and specific sexual encounters. One man explained why he thought skills were important for magnificent sex:

> It's having a lot of options, so that there's lots of choices. It's kind of like to be a great artist you need to have lots of technical skills so that you can make sure that what you're drawing or painting is exactly what you want.

Having a body of knowledge and certain technical skills could be helpful in building confidence, allowing a person to relax and be present during sex. Knowing some basic sexual techniques could be compared to learning a few social dance moves (e.g., turns, spins): From there, it becomes possible to explore, be creative and improvise.

Many different types of skills were mentioned during interviews, including touch, kissing, massage, oral sex, manual sex and intercourse; however, there were no particular recommendations or specifics about *how* to do these things, only that skills in those areas could be useful. Likewise, optimal sexual experiences may require a good, basic understanding of anatomy. As one woman explained:

> [Knowing] what you can do and can't do and how it feels . . . what parts of the body are so sensitive they have to be touched very carefully and what parts can take more pressure, and how you can increase the pressure as the person is getting more turned on.

Other sexual skills that were mentioned included those related to intensity, style, speed and repetition, as well as an internal sense of timing and rhythm. "The ability to move your body how you want it to move", explained one man.

A few individuals expressed their preference for some very specific and specialized sexual activities (e.g., fetishes, bondage, flogging, fisting); in those cases, knowledge and skills related to their particular preferences were essential (e.g., how to safely tie up a partner, appropriate pre-fisting nail care). One woman described how her husband's techniques contributed to optimal sexual experiences:

> Spanking is a skill . . . I basically taught him how to spank me. How I want it. And that's probably why I love it so much with him and not so much with other people because you really do have to hit a person's rhythm, do you know what I mean? And give it the way that they want it.

Technical skills were consistently de-emphasized in favour of other important contributors (e.g., sensitivity, attentiveness, responsiveness, communication, focus, connection). One woman explained: "[Skills] often shorten your
journey between bad sex and great sex but it's not necessary because sex con-
tains its own wonder." Virtually everyone who mentioned skills also emphasized that these techniques could be learned, whether from workshops, books
or simple experimentation with a partner (or even alone). Or, as one person,
explained:

> I think the skills are more mental skills and emotional skills than
> they are physical skills because if you have the empathy and you
> have the desire to connect, if you're paying attention to the feed-
> back you're getting from your partner, nonverbal as well as verbal,
> that'll give you the physical skills you need.

Skills Unique to the Partner(s) in the Encounter

Perhaps the most important aspect of developing sexual knowledge and skills
is knowing how to tailor these techniques to specific partners rather than
applying them generically and indiscriminately to all sexual partners. Extraordinary lovers focused on learning together, making changes and fine tuning
their existing knowledge to the needs of each individual sexual partner. One
man said, "My experience with everyone is different. You may be sexually
competent, I think, with one person and totally inept with another. So it's
almost like you start all over again." In fact, most people who mentioned
technical skills also added that doing the same thing to everyone was likely to
get in the way of optimal sexual experiences rather than bring them about.

Some specifically said that using exactly the same skills on every partner
was more likely to lead to bad sex than good sex. One person explained, "The
skill is not something you just go out and do the same thing to everybody, but
it's, it's knowing what the other, being able to read or to ask what the other
person really likes."

Although they highlight the importance of sexual skills as contributors to
optimal sexual experiences, extraordinary lovers in this study felt differently.
Most said that skills and techniques were largely irrelevant because the
very best sex "is not mechanical, it's in your mind", as one man put it. They
explained that although it was important to learn basic techniques and
anatomy, it was far *more* important to learn about one's self and one's partners
and to communicate. Techniques per se could not bring about magnificent

sex but they could certainly help to create a solid foundation on which to build. Having a wide repertoire of skills gave people the creativity, confidence and flexibility they needed to be able to create the specific kinds of sexual experiences they wanted.

Many emphasized the absurdity of magazine and book recommendations (e.g., "21 moves guaranteed to make his thighs go up in flames"). As one man said:

> So there's not a like magic great skill sex. Great sex skill where if you just learn this one skill and use it then you're bound to get to great sex. And there's not this one activity. You just tie somebody up just right and that'll be perfect and then they'll really, you know, no rope burns on one hand, just . . . doesn't hurt too much but just enough. It's not like that. It's about . . . being able to be yourself and be empathetic and be connected and to be, you know, all at the same time.

This idea cannot be emphasized enough: Techniques used in isolation without attention to individual, interpersonal and contextual elements *will not* create magnificent sex. This is the key distinction between the sexual skills described here versus sexual techniques as described in sex tip blogs. The idea is not to learn to cook by memorizing a bunch of different recipes and serving them to guests indiscriminately, regardless of tastes and preferences (and allergies). Rather, one learns the fundamentals of different cooking techniques, the theory behind why certain ingredients go together and then flavour and season according to taste. The skills, techniques and knowledge of anatomy provide a solid foundation to build on, to elaborate and be creative, to customize and experiment.

The most crucial skills required for optimal sexual experiences are the capacities for communication and especially mutual empathy in general, as well as during sexual encounters.

As such, we will devote an entire chapter (11) to empathic communication and its pivotal role in creating magnificent sex.

9
QUALITIES OF THE RELATIONSHIP

What is great sex? An older woman replied, "My husband." She added:

> It's not a technique to be a good lover. It's an, it's an involvement. It's an acceptance of ourselves and of our partners, uh, open-mindedness, uh, ability communi-, to communicate what we really need and want and uh, trust that the other person is willing to hang in there and understand and do it [pause]. So it's a whole relationship evolution rather than a sexual technique. *And I could explain to ten other men what my husband does that turns me on and if they did it, I don't know that I'd be turned on, I think I wouldn't.*

For some extraordinary lovers, the concept of magnificent sex could not be separated out from the relationship in which it occurs, such is the degree of overlap. Optimal sexual experiences were not a matter of techniques or tricks that just *anyone* could employ but were firmly embedded in the matrix of their connections with another person(s). The relationships that they described varied tremendously (e.g., number of years together, sexual orientation, open/monogamous) but there did appear to be a core set of qualities, characteristics and skills that were common across participants and made an enormous contribution to the calibre of their sexual experiences. One of our happiest and most encouraging findings may be that magnificent sex is possible not only in the flush of a new relationship but may grow with a partner of 30, 40 or even 50+ years.

A few caveats here too: Not all of these contributors were present in any one relationship, nor were all present at the same time, nor were all necessary for each individual. Rather, different qualities might emerge as being crucial in different relationships at different times. Please think of these elements as a buffet and not a *menu fixe*.

Empathy: The Overarching Factor that Makes Everything Else Possible

The role of empathy as a contributor to optimal sexual experiences could not be overstated. Empathy was not only a component of optimal sexual experiences but it was the overarching and underlying factor that created magnificent sex. It was the *"sine qua non"* with regard to relationship qualities – an important contributor on its own but also one that helped to facilitate virtually every other relationship quality. In other words, empathy was crucial for improving the quality of sexual experiences directly; it also helped foster trust, communication and safety that were, in their turn, helpful in bringing about magnificent sex.

What we are talking about here is expressive and receptive verbal communication as well as the power of giving and receiving touch in ways that communicate that one is now virtually living in the other's world, or as a participant worded it, "feeling into the other's space." It is touching in such a way as to feel and penetrate metaphorically the person within. It is also about the willingness to let oneself be touched so as to be felt. In contrast, imagine the way one's body responds when bracing for an injection or a blood test.

The word empathy can be difficult to define and it has been used to mean everything from trying to understand someone else's perspective all the way to self-transcendence and total immersion in the other's experience. The level of empathy we encountered among those we interviewed went far beyond the way this term is usually defined in the couples therapy literature. It is certainly a much higher level of empathy than is found in mainstream clinical psychology (cf., Hart, 1997, 1999, 2000; Mahrer, 2004; Mahrer, Boulet & Fairweather, 1994).

Extraordinary lovers talked about the importance of sensitivity, "real listening" and "paying attention to the little things". One woman summarized this as, "Being able to listen, to respond, to organize information, to recognize even if you're not told, that one kind of touch elicits a certain response in your partner and another does not." Feeling into another person's space, being on the same wavelength, getting inside the other person's being (metaphorically) or sharing a "headspace" were other perspectives on the concept.

Although we are mentioning empathy here, its role is so central to all aspects of creating magnificent sex that an entire chapter is devoted to it.

Shared Beliefs and Attitudes – Especially about Prioritizing Sexuality in Relationships

In order to create and cultivate magnificent sexual encounters within a relationship, it is important not only for individuals to care about it but also that their beliefs and attitudes be shared, or at least compatible, with those of their partners. Each of the lovers has to be interested in bringing about those types of experiences and in creating the types of relationships in which magnificent sex is enabled. An older female sex therapist described the power of jointly-held beliefs:

> I keep going back to that wonderful film that Masters and Johnson showed us of a person who was, uh, quadruple amputee and her husband and how wonderful they, how wonderfully they described his sex life and came away with, you know anybody, who has an interest and an interested partner can have good sex. So I sort of feel that way about it, I always have. *So, um, I think if two people have a mind to have great sex with each other, they probably will have it.*

Extraordinary lovers prioritize and cherish their relational bonds. They told us repeatedly how much their partners mattered to them and reinforced this message with countless examples. They put these beliefs into practice by consistently putting in effort, demonstrating commitment and bringing intentionality to the relationship. One woman, who told us she had been raised in an emotionally cold household, described deliberately working on physical affection in her marriage:

> But I do think that the affection, I think that the touching outside of sex – the connecting outside of sex – 'How was your day at work?' You know, I think all of that is really important to building the relationship, which you have to have to have great sex.

We would not usually connect gentle shoulder rubs directly with sex but there is a clear link here – putting effort into the relationship on a daily basis makes it the kind of relationship in which magnificent sex is possible, if not frequent! The same may be true for sending text messages during the day, remembering to take the garbage out or picking up a favorite treat from the grocery store. No one of these behaviours is likely to lead to magnificent sex but all of them strengthen the connection and communicate to a partner the value and primacy of the relationship. Another woman described the ongoing process of building her relationships with her partners:

> And I have great sex with them because I care about them and they're great human beings and I don't have any expectations when I call one over and I say: 'Well, you know, let's get together today. You know, it would be really great just have a drink.' And I'm like: 'That'd be awesome.' And we go and we have a drink, and if a drink is all we have, then that's okay. That's not great sex, but it's still building our relationship.

This same degree of caring and attention that these individuals brought to their relationships was also turned towards the sexual experiences in those relationships. Wanting optimal sexual intimacy to happen and setting up the necessary conditions at a variety of different levels was an ongoing priority. One person explained:

> I think that requires, you know, both people wanting that to happen, making it a priority, uh, setting aside time and, um, being able to relax into it or to play into it or to get invested in it. And I think most people, like other parts of their lives, um, fall into, you know, their habits and their patterns and, um, and are busy and pulled in other directions and so for most people, I think it doesn't go that way. Just like I think most people don't become great *cooks* or, um, or great whatever it is, you know, hobbyists, you know, they just kind of do it how they do it and some people do, kind of, get invested and they do get to the greater place. I also think it's really hard to get to the greater place *alone*, I think your partner needs to be into it also, so whereas I might become a great pianist because I devote a lot of my time to playing piano, um, now, you know, my partner would also have to devote a lot of time to playing, um, at being a sexual partner so I think that it doesn't happen, um, as often. I think it's harder.

This quotation neatly illustrates the bizarre role that sex occupies in Western culture. We would not generally expect that a person would become proficient at something without focused effort and time (e.g., piano playing, marathon running) and yet many of us expect that magnificent sex will just materialize out of the blue. Optimal sexual experiences may represent an additional challenge in that both individuals need to work together and so attitudes and beliefs in this area must be shared. However, the rewards may be significant. Just as individuals working together on non-sexual projects may create something exponentially better than one person alone (e.g., Lennon and McCartney), so too may sexual partners create something spectacular between them.

Several individuals talked about the differences between work and effort, emphasizing the latter rather than the former. One man described why consistent energy and attention were necessary:

> So it's not the, it's not that, you know, connection and intimacy are constantly increasing, it's that, you know, in a world that sort of causes it to decrease every now and then, sometimes you need to re-build in order to come back to the place where you were the day before . . .

Anyone who has taken high school science may understand this as a kind of entropy – that is, the tendency of things to decline into disorder. Houseplants die, laundry piles up, the number of e-mails in our inbox grows unless we consistently put in time and effort. It seems that relationships and sex are no different. One man shared some very good advice he had received about the attitude required for a strong marriage and for magnificent sex:

> I've read a number of things and, you know, talked to other people and it's, it's kind of been the whole guidelines but, the best advice I ever heard, um, was from a guy who had been married for fifty-some years and he said – and I think this applies to sex as much as anything else – but he said that, that *the secret to a good relationship was if you made every move and every decision based upon your partner's happiness, you couldn't go wrong. The trick was you both had to do that. And I think that works very well with sex.*

This comment may be the epitome of what it takes to make erotic intimacy flourish, although as this man indicated, each lover has to commit to prioritizing the other's best interests or it will not fly.

Wanting sex to happen, prioritizing it, planning and setting aside time all helped to build both the relationship and future sexual encounters. In many ways, this may be one of the more fundamental contributors to magnificent sex because as extraordinary lovers repeatedly emphasized, optimal sexual experiences were predicated to a much greater degree on good management than on good luck. All of the other contributors identified in this chapter require both people to work towards, learn, grow, develop and maintain. This is not necessarily difficult or aversive but it does require effort, beginning with a choice to engage. The problem for individuals and therapists in dealing with low desire is that we often realize rather quickly that the absence of sexual desire on one person's part is linked with the absence of overall effort on the part of the partner.

Creating a Sexually Conducive Interpersonal Atmosphere

"Your relationship is being articulated in everything you do," explained one person. The atmosphere of the relationship is like the weather or the emotional climate – the backdrop against which everything else becomes possible, although it may not be as obvious as other factors. Or, as another person put it, "Sex is more outside the bedroom than it is in." (This is not an idea that we see articulated in many places but certainly an important one.)

A sense of trust was, for many, a necessary prerequisite for magnificent sex, whether the relationship in question lasted 35 years or one night. "Trust is basic," said one woman. Extraordinary lovers defined trust across multiple levels: physically, emotionally, spiritually, financially, etc. Some individuals had experienced abuse, neglect or trauma in their history, which made this contributor particularly salient. But one of the most valuable takeaways from their stories is that trust in others *could* be regained and at incredibly deep levels. Others characterized their relationships as having an abiding sense of security within the relationship, a "safety in the essence". As one man said, "I mean, there's an incredible sense of trust with your partner, there's a sense of security. And both of those might just be a different way of saying 'peace', right?" Non-judgmental acceptance from a partner was a huge component of creating a sense of safety. One man described this as, "Knowing that whatever is there is okay. It might not be comfortable, but it's okay." Respect and consideration between partners was often built on the foundation of trust and safety. The security that couples felt with one another made it possible for them to be joyful and lighthearted, to learn and grow and explore and make mistakes.

Extraordinary lovers offered differing opinions on how long it would take to create that level of trust. Some felt that it was possible to develop instantly. In a few cases, they described a feeling of automatic trust with the partner with whom they had their greatest sexual encounters. Others felt that it took more time and communication to establish boundaries and clarify limits. These people described the growth of trust and safety over multiple years in a partnership (though not always a traditional, monogamous partnership). The idea of falling "in trust" with someone is not an idea that we see in the mainstream discourse about sex and some of the sex therapists we interviewed did not believe that this was even possible.

Almost everyone who highlighted the importance of relational qualities in creating magnificent sex brought up respect and consideration. For the majority, respect was such an integral relational quality that without it, optimal sexual experiences were simply not possible. Extraordinary lovers talked about respecting their partners as individuals and honouring their sexualities. They told us it was important to be respectful of needs, desires and feelings, even when these were not commonly-held, and to obey limits, boundaries and agreements even, or perhaps especially, when it was a challenge to do so. They emphasized that the respect must be absolutely mutual between partners. The depth of this respect was described by some as "profound". One man described respect in his relationships, also highlighting the role of communication: "We're not going to assume that just because I want XYZ you'd want XYZ, 'cause we've talked about that. We know what letters of the alphabet are okay and which ones are not."

Consideration and respect were often mentioned in the same sentence and each seemed to flow naturally from the other. A partner whom one respects is always treated with consideration, both sexually and non-sexually. Several individuals described their past or current partners as being more concerned for the other than for themselves. An older man who had been married over 40 years explained the impact of respect and consideration on the marriage:

> Partner sex is aided by having a partner, who is able to contract life with . . . So that they're able to make deals like, when I say 'I'm going to meet you at five o'clock', it means five or five after but not seven-thirty. In other words, I'm going to be really pleased when I meet you, and not pissed off. And that grows into all the other facts of the relationship which, if it's neat and kind and pleasant, gives it a chance to mushroom into great sex.

He later added, "And, um, I don't *ever* remember coming home with the feeling that I'd rather not be doing this."

Walking in the door and feeling unhappy with your partner really does make magnificent sex an uphill battle (and probably far less likely). But how often do we talk about the connection between being late and having magnificent sex? If, as one individual said, our relationship is being articulated in everything we do, then even small gestures matter, which can either build towards wonderful sex or away from it. Magnificent sex is not just facilitated by the actions and statements that occur in the 15 minutes immediately preceding the act but in everything that makes up the overall atmosphere of the relationship.

Strong Feelings Within the Individual and Between Partners

Extraordinary lovers often spontaneously made the distinction between "hot" sex and truly magnificent sex. They explained that it was the combination of the physical with emotional intimacy and connection that made the difference. Physical sensations alone were not enough to bring about "great sex". As one person explained, "You can't have great sex unless there's emotions involved." Or, as another woman put it, "I can have a great physical experience with my vibrator. Um, I, for me to consider it great sex, um, with a partner, it's got to be more than just physically satisfying." Strong feelings between partners were the difference (and the reason that great lovers did not just stick to their vibrators).

We must pause to note that the contribution of strong feelings to optimal sexual experiences was important even for consensually non-monogamous individuals who had sex outside of their primary relationships. These types of feelings could be cultivated in many different types of relationships – and were. Some participants only experienced magnificent sex with a spouse or long-term partner and some expressed doubt that they could ever have sex of this calibre with anyone else. As one man explained, "I'm not knocking swinging. I mean, it's a lot of fun, we've met a lot of fun people. But my wife is better." And several individuals reported having magnificent sex with friends or play partners – people with whom they had close, warm friendships but who were not their primary partners or romantic partners.

In talking about the importance of feelings within a relationship, two broad categories of emotions emerged. Extraordinary lovers told us about all kinds of different feelings that they experienced *with* their partners, in the presence of other persons, as part of their connection together. They also talked about the emotions that they experienced *towards* the other person, feelings that they carried around inside of them like a lantern – warm, glowing feelings that were always with them no matter how great the physical distance from their partners.

Intrapsychic "Lantern" Feelings

Extraordinary lovers emphasized how much they cared for their partners, and how this caring made magnificent sexual experiences possible. They expressed liking for their partners, appreciation, positive regard, respect and support. One man described the bond with his sexual partners: "They care about me, I care about them. We have one another's best interests at heart . . . That even sounds too crude. We want to hold one another tenderly."

One word that we expected to hear relatively often was the one word that was used only rarely: love. In fact, the word came up only a handful of times across the entire set of interviews. Although participants used all the words that are usually connected with the concept of "love", that word in particular was almost never used. However, perhaps this was a deliberate choice on the part of these individuals. Instead of using an ambiguous, vague and overused word like "love", perhaps they were deliberately trying to be more nuanced and precise with their language. In fact, it seemed that they distilled love down to its constituent parts. The need to redefine simple words or to consider them in greater depth is a surprising and unintended outcome of this research, although perhaps it is one of our more important findings and one that deserves further attention in the research and clinical realms.

Extraordinary lovers talked about having a sense of goodwill and sensitivity towards their partners, as well as an interest in their partners as people, and feeling curious about them. One man described having, "A kind of profound respect for the other person's experience and a fundamental curiosity about them and a really open desire to explore them." They felt positively about their partners, even towards those with whom they were no longer in a relationship. (Contrary to the tired trope of expressing resentment or hatred towards an ex-partner, extraordinary lovers often spoke highly of their former lovers and in respectful tones.)

Acceptance was a major piece of this caring, making room for all aspects of their partners. Our participants could see their partners' good qualities and their challenges and could appreciate the entire package rather than put their partners on pedestals. One man elaborated:

> I heard somewhere, you reach a point in a relationship with somebody when you love them not in spite of their flaws and not precisely because of their flaws but they are them and that's all part of what they are and you love that. And so in that sense, the flaws are as uniquely them as the virtues . . . I never knew that I was going to find that. And that was the condition of acceptance I always yearned for when I was a kid and couldn't get.

Acceptance, like many other concepts identified in this research, is a relational component that can, with diligent attention and effort, get better and better.

For many, the relationships in which they first experienced magnificent sex were among the first relationships in which they felt truly, deeply accepted. This level of acceptance is part of what made it possible for individuals to be authentic and vulnerable with their partners, and part of what allowed them to jettison old ways of thinking and venture into the unknown.

For a few people, "love" was identified as necessary for optimal sexual experiences. One woman said simply, "When love's involved, it's the best." For such individuals, good sex might be possible without love but not magnificent sex. One man explained the cyclical nature between sex and love:

> That's one of the things about the English language. You know, you talk about making love and, yeah, in one respect, that's exactly what it does because I believe that, that good sex, great sex increases love in the relationship, or between the partners anyway.

However, most seemed to believe that real, genuine liking towards a partner was more important for magnificent sex than loving. One woman explained: "I like all of my lovers . . . I'm friends with them and I care about them as human beings. And I have great sex with them because I care about them and they're great human beings." A man said that he wanted to have sex with "one or more partners that I truly enjoy as people. I don't have to be in love, but I really need to like them as people."

Consider that when we talk about magnificent sex, we do not usually talk about the "liking" part of the relationship. We may say that we love our partners but we rarely tell them that we like them. This is reflected in social beliefs about how we spend our leisure hours; we will often make time for work colleagues or friends but not the most important persons in our lives. There is a distinct danger in writing emotional IOUs to a primary partner that is not obviously apparently on a week-to-week or month-to-month basis but becomes obvious, and sometimes very painfully so, on a year-to-year basis. The presumption that we would not choose to spend more time with our partners if we could or that we do not enjoy them as people (e.g., *Modern Family*) all stand in stark contrast to the statements made by our participants and the liking, caring, goodwill and acceptance that they treasured.

Shared Feelings (Interpersonal)

In addition to the emotions that extraordinary lovers felt for their partners that were experienced within, they also talked about shared feelings that tied and connected them to their partners that were built and expanded on together. This connection involved physical, intellectual, spiritual and emotional bonds. "Emotionally entwined" is how one person described these feelings, while another person described the connection as "bridging a gap". One man, who regularly participated in swinging with his wife of 20+ years, was asked what made sex so great with her in contrast to the sex he had with partners he met through swinging. He explained:

> If I didn't love her, the sex wouldn't be the same. I mean, it's just, it's the feeling I get when I hold her as compared to the feeling you get when you hold somebody else that you don't love. It's just a closeness . . . you feel like, you feel like one as compared to maybe feeling like two with somebody else.

Extraordinary lovers emphasized the closeness, warmth and nurturance they felt within their relationships; they described their connections with their partners as "gentle" and "tender". By their descriptions, it seemed that many savoured the time they spent in the presence of their partners. An older woman stated, "We feel good about each other. When we're finished making love we're, and it's the way I feel about my husband, too, I feel happy to be with him. I'm glad I'm there with him." Another woman explained, "Um, if I go a while without having sex with my husband I start feeling lonely, I start losing that sense that, you know, he's my guy, we're walking through life together . . ." Magnificent sex requires strong feelings between partners but sex can also build on and enhance those feelings. Sex can bind a relationship together and enhance a sense of togetherness or being on the same team.

Lest readers begin to think that we are veering too far away from sex and closer to the realm of Hallmark greeting cards, we can also happily report that some also saw chemistry and attraction as important aspects of a relationship in which magnificent sex might be possible. Extraordinary lovers talked about being physically, emotionally and mentally turned on by their partners. As one person said, it's about, "Being excited about each other as people." Another man explained that for magnificent sex to be possible in a relationship, he needed to feel "moved" by his partners: "They had to do something special for you." One woman described the path from mutual attraction to magnificent sex:

> For me, it's usually, there's been an attraction that's gone on for a while and then, and then, you know it and you've talked about it and you know you're clearly both aware of it and you both intentionally decide that that is what you wanted. And then you go ahead and act on it [laughs].

People described these kinds of relationships as "emotionally charged", passionate, intense and intimate. Several talked about having an ongoing crush on their partners. One woman explained: "And I really want somebody to want me. You know, to kind of know me, to be infatuated with me in some way or have a crush or really have that desire to get closer to me." Feelings of freshness, excitement or energy in some cases had lasted for years. One woman who had been married for many years talked about the passion she felt for her husband:

> When he walks in a room, my breath catches. Um, that, um, and I'll find myself, he's done the same thing, I'll, like, see him in a crowd and not recognize him and I'll be going, 'God, oh man, he's hot. Oh. I'm married to him' [laughing]. Not realizing I'm checking out my own husband. Um, that, that sort of freshness and, um, you know, kind of warm, mushy, you know, I've got a, the guy I've got a crush on is interested in me feeling has stayed.

In many cases, when asked what environmental contributors were important for optimal sexual experiences, participants would state if passion and intensity were present, environmental contributors were largely irrelevant. A few had experienced magnificent sex in seemingly uncomfortable situations (e.g., in a back alley, while camping) because of the intensity of feelings with their partners. (We would like to take this moment to express our shared skepticism that camping might result in optimal sexual experiences.)

The idea of having a crush on your long-term partner stands in contrast to pop culture representations of long-term relationships, specifically, the assumption that attraction usually fades or disappears. Consider characters like Barney on *How I Met Your Mother*, who spent their time jumping from one partner to the next and who break off relationships if the intensity fades. This pessimism is also sometimes seen in the world of couples therapy, where well-meaning therapists warn couples not to expect the same calibre of sex later in the relationship that they recall from the "honeymoon phase". What might ensue if we relinquished this belief? What might we aspire towards instead? We could refuse to compromise, refuse to settle. Perhaps instead of searching endlessly for the next big crush, we could put serious, deliberate effort into the relationship and see where "a kind of profound curiosity" about our partners might lead.

Exploring Together

With empathy and communication, shared priorities around the relationship and magnificent sex, and against the backdrop of safety, respect and trust, participants were well-equipped to go exploring together. Being willing and excited to experiment, learn and grow together were important qualities of relationships in which magnificent sex was possible. Extraordinary lovers valued the chance to learn more about their partners and themselves through sex. No matter how long the relationship, many felt that there was still much to be discovered and did not take their existing knowledge as given or as final. In the words of one person: "The sense that whatever you're doing, you know, the sense of what you're doing is new, even if you've done it before." Such individuals talked enthusiastically about venturing into the unknown and taking risks with their long-term partners. An older man described his 40-plus year marriage as, "A life of sexual exploration and adventure and excitement." His wife, who was interviewed separately, stated: "I think it's a wiser path to understand the mystery of our sexuality and go into it with that attitude, uh, between the partners of 'let's explore.' Let's explore both of our fantasies and see where this leads us."

The word "experimentation" in this context was defined quite differently by the people we interviewed compared to the way this word is often used colloquially. Rather than emphasizing novelty for its own sake, extraordinary lovers talked about experimenting in order to learn more about themselves, their partners and sex itself. They talked about venturing into the unknown and taking risks. However, this word was also not defined in the way that "sexual risks" are usually defined in the research literature (e.g., unintended pregnancy, STIs). A risk could be learning more about oneself or one's partner, being authentic and vulnerable with a trusted other or expanding one's sexual boundaries. Risks could mean taking the chance of saying or doing something that is unknown, that might be challenging and that might create some discomfort without knowing how it will turn out. But what might be possible if we leaned into this discomfort? Realistically, can there be substantial and meaningful growth in life in any other way?

10
RELATIONAL QUALITIES IN-THE-MOMENT

If the previous chapter was focused on important relationship characteristics which contributed in general to magnificent sex, it might be of use to conceptualize this chapter as about the relationship *in motion* during sex.

Optimal Sexual Experiences Are Always Consensual

The contribution of consent to magnificent sex was, for most extraordinary lovers, an afterthought. They would often mention casually, "Oh, and of course it's consensual", thereby reflecting how obvious and fundamental it was to them. The implication was that consent was necessary but definitely not sufficient by itself.

The importance of this finding cannot be overemphasized in the aftermath of the "Me Too" controversy: When individuals are arguing about consent, it is inevitably in the context of coercive sex or at best, very bad sex. In magnificent sex, it is a given that consent is essential. In American society, merely assuming consent is the default option. The American discourse about the possibility of instituting affirmative consent (that is, the idea of actively expressing consent rather than taking consent for granted, when there is silence during initiation and sexual preliminaries) has been quite negative. The assumption has been that having to talk about consent would ruin the mood. It is noteworthy that Canadian law has required affirmative consent since 1983 and it has not led to diminishing sexual overtures.

One man explained how ongoing discussions about consent were woven into his polyamorous relationships:

> What can I do to ensure that I have great sex? The preplanning for me is . . . having people in my life that I connect with in a sexual way and having really clear communication between myself and my partners. You know, what's sort of our attitude for sex with each other, what's our attitude for sex with other people. If I'm walking down the street and have the opportunity for sex in an alley because I light someone's cigarette the right way outside of a bar, you know is that . . . sort of having all the logistical . . . would these things be consensual between myself and the important relationships in my life beforehand is a way to, I think, ensure that I will be having great sex.

This quotation illustrates both the specificity of consent and the breadth of the concept – not just consent to a single sexual encounter but consent to a broader approach to sex and sexuality within the relationship(s). For extraordinary lovers, consent was an ongoing conversation about the who, what, where, when and how of sexual experiences, and a much more complex idea than whether it is permissible to insert tab A into slot B. It certainly contradicts popular misconceptions of BDSM (e.g., *Fifty Shades of Grey*) but also stands in contrast to the conventional sex education approaches to teaching consent, which is often depicted as an "on/off" switch – either someone does or does not consent to a sexual activity. Couples who take this approach to their committed relationships may find themselves confused and upset as years go on, needs evolve and circumstances change. Optimal sexual experiences may require couples to revisit their respective assumptions about any unspoken contracts on a regular basis and flesh out the details of what they agree to sexually in order to avoid misunderstandings, boundary violations and hurt feelings.

Mutuality and Reciprocity

Like consent, mutuality was a concept defined much more broadly by the people we spoke with than typical and went far beyond the physical aspects of sex. They applied this idea to all levels of a sexual encounter: mutual feelings of connection, respect, desire, arousal, satisfaction, investment, etc. Mutuality and reciprocity often were mentioned as an aside during interviews while participants were in the midst of discussing other, important contributors to optimal sexual experiences. They would add something like, "But *of course* my partner also needs to be thinking/feeling/doing that" to clarify whatever points they were originally making. For many, mutuality seemed to be woven into their definition of optimal sexual experiences. One man explained, "You can't have a, a great sex . . . as I understand it, without the mutuality."

For many, mutuality did *not* refer only or even primarily to physical sensations; instead, it was often focused on emotional needs. For example, they talked about mutual levels of embodiment and connection during the event. "Knowing that the other is as invested as you are in this moment" is how one person put it, or having an "enormous level of synchronicity" said another. One man explained his definition of mutuality:

> I've mentioned the extreme degree of mutuality and by that, I mean, I don't mean that we're like, you know, experiencing the same thing at the same time but I'm as focused and I think my wife is as focused on partner experience as they are in self experience.

Mutuality wasn't defined by perfect sameness and matching in terms of behaviours. Many engaged in trades with their partners, for example, "You enjoy this sexual behaviour but I do not – I will do it for you and you will do something different for me." Mutuality referred to a sense of equality, mutual investment and enjoyment. One man explained, "They don't have to mirror, mirrors of liking, uh, the same experience but they have to like participating in it."

Reciprocity and fairness were key pieces in this definition of mutuality. One person commented, "It isn't something one does *to* a person, it's something one does *with* a person." In talking about what it takes to make a sexual experience magnificent, many emphasized the need for exchange, going back and forth, fluidity and ease. One older man stated, "It should be reciprocal, give-and-take rather than take-and-give." Another person said:

> I think there has to be a sense of initiative on the part of someone and it's usually best when that initiative really passes back and forth. That is, I'm making love to you, you're making love to me, and it can go back and forth in in the blink of an eye.

Some described less-than-optimal experiences with partners who could not grasp its importance. One woman told us about a relationship that did not involve a feeling of give and take and compared the situation to being operated "like a pinball machine". Notwithstanding her partner's expertise at genital manipulation, she was struck by his lack of attention to the woman attached to the genitals. This stands in contrast to romance novels that often represent an "ideal" sexual encounter as one in which a female character is the passive recipient of an endless chain of orgasms and derives no pleasure from taking a more active role in pleasuring her partner (Cabrera & Ménard, 2012; Ménard & Cabrera, 2011).

Mutuality and reciprocity go far beyond the physical; they also speak to the importance of looking at the deeper values that are often driving our responses to sexual encounters. Is the real issue that he does not want to perform oral sex or is that her expectations around fairness have been violated? Is the problem that she is not aroused/lubricated enough or is it that his level of arousal greatly exceeds hers and she feels left out of the sexual encounter? Perhaps absolute mirroring of behaviours is not the issue but rather it is lack of fairness and investment that are the real problems.

Eroticism

Extraordinary lovers stressed how important it was to define the erotic by and for themselves. No particular sex acts or behaviours were deemed universally erotic across participants. Eroticism was not a generic or abstract concept for these individuals; rather it was as distinctive as fingerprints. In fact, the uniqueness and unpredictability of their definitions was deeply compelling. Individuals talked about the erotic qualities of the seduction process, the contact, touch and the energy exchanged between partners. An older man described how his best sexual encounters often begin:

> The connection, the glance, the, the recognition, the mutual recognition that this is a sexual moment is complete and mutual and spontaneous and sort of sparks the interaction. Then there follows, once that awareness has come, some time of, like dancing around this sort of final conclusion like approaching and withdrawing and describing the outlines of the experience through gentle exploration in various ways . . . The really peak experiences always include that exploration and the, sort of a regard, a glance, oblique approaches, engaging more and more of the other person. Sort of begins to spin a web of excitement . . . out in space and time around you, around it through the two of us and then it kind of takes the energy from not just our lives but the things that are happening beyond us but at that time, and pulls that energy into a sexual moment and makes it really more powerful and exciting.

The role of eye contact as a sexual behaviour was often first mentioned when participants talked about eroticism. Extraordinary lovers talked about catching their partners' eyes or holding a look a little longer than necessary. Magnificent erotic encounters could begin in very subtle but meaningful ways. One man explained:

> It can be the touching of fingers across the table or when you ride in the car, you could touch the other, I could touch my partner's leg, for instance, and that's the beginning of what eventually, within a reasonable time-span leads to us having, making love.

Building anticipation, prolonging the sexual encounter and engaging in sexual teasing could all enhance the eroticism of a sexual encounter and bring it to greater heights. Participants talked about feelings of anticipation during the sexual experience and described deliberately building their partners' arousal for its own sake and stoking desire. As an older man put it, "What I really loved was, was the doing, and the being, and, and how long can we just be *in* this state of trust and responsiveness." Another man equated great sex with "great plateau". An older man explained why setting aside sufficient time was crucial in the creation of optimal sexual experiences:

> The more aroused you are . . . and sometimes – it depends on ability to put off the intercourse for – you have to have enough time to put it off for a while, for a couple of hours to do all kinds of things beforehand is just fantastic. Whether it's bathing or showering or dancing or taking each other's clothes off and dancing together nude or, um, whatever it is. So then when you finally get to the point of actually penetrating her, *oh*, it just is . . . [pauses] that's where we were going with all of that, kind of the culmination of everything that led up to it. But on the other hand, everything that led up to it is equally as important as sexual intercourse.

The role of eroticism speaks to the importance of redefining and expanding our beliefs about a "typical" sexual encounter. If sex can begin with a glance or a touching of fingers or even, as one male participant described, a heightened awareness of a partner's perfume, we need to rethink the "line drive" model (Castleman, 2004) so often depicted in the media and reified in self-help books (that is, the idea that sex proceeds directly from kissing to touching to manual/oral stimulation to intercourse in a straight line). Magnificent sex may require that we slow down and build on our capacity to notice the subtleties, the tiny behaviours that do not seem, at first glance, to be connected to the sexual. It also brings us back to the importance of intentionality, both in planning and making room for the sexual encounter, and during the sex itself. Magnificent sex is a conscious choice, not an accident. It is deliberate.

This element, eroticism, struck our research team because in some ways, it was the first element of magnificent sex that was, at least superficially, directly about "sex". One of our fellow researchers exclaimed, "Finally! The *sexy* part of sex." We are left wondering about the extent to which our studies have captured not only the elements of optimal sexual experience but perhaps also the components and structure of all peak experiences – save for the distinctly erotic.

Being Swept up, Connected and Lost Together

Extraordinary lovers talked about feeling fully embodied and present while connected and feeling part of a joint experience. One person explained:

> While I'm having great sex what we're doing is . . . focusing on connecting to my body and another person, um . . . trying to get – sometimes it feels like inside their brain or inside their being and you have some types of, some type of, um, connection together.

Many identified this as the factor that elevated good physical experiences to magnificent sexual experiences. This connection went beyond the physical to involve every aspect of the person – mind, body and spirit. A younger woman described how a sense of connection could elevate sex from mundane to optimal:

> We have an intimate connection which brings us to a different level. So there's always, there's always more than one thing going on. It isn't just that we both want to fuck, it's that we both want to fuck and both really vibe on the same level of something else.

One woman explained what she thought was necessary to create such a connection:

> You have to be willing to fall in love with that person for the duration of your connection to them, in some form or another. I'm not talking Hallmark roses and cheesy music. And then you have to be both willing and able, and I think that's where we get stuck in our culture, to gracefully fall out of love when the appropriate timing is complete. That timing could be, you know, 'I'm going to fall in love with you for the next half hour because we're going to sit here and

fuck' or, 'I'm going to hook my fortunes up to your wagon-train and see how long it takes us down the road.'

This type of intense connection helped to create a sense of intimacy and privacy in which the rest of the world was excluded and the lovers could revel in their own self-contained bubble. Extraordinary lovers talked about losing themselves to the sexual experience and losing touch with the rest of the world. One sex therapist recalled a scene from the movie *Four Weddings and a Funeral*, where a couple found themselves so wrapped up in a sexual encounter that they failed to notice the protagonist, stuck in the bathroom of their hotel room. He stated, "It's just clear the two of them are just *lost* in the experience . . . They don't notice anything, they're just oblivious, now that's great sex!" One woman described this feeling as, "Two people being in the right headspace at the right time together." This experience was often bidirectional – feelings of connection helped to bring about a sense of being lost together, which reinforced and built the connection between partners.

The joy of getting swept up, connecting intensely to a sexual partner and getting lost in the moment is an aspect of optimal sexual experiences that sex therapists hear about regularly, but recollections of it are often relegated to sad stories about the couple's past. What may be missing is the active role that partners can play in cultivating this and trying to bring this about purposefully. This is one of the elements that gets lost in the focus on the physical and the behavioural. Creating connection to another person on multiple levels speaks to the importance to sex being primarily "between the ears" rather than "between the legs". If you are really connecting to the other person, lost in the moment together, does it matter what the genitals are doing? Sexual connection is often presented as the happy by-product of early relationship bliss rather than a state that can be deliberately nurtured. Articles in magazines and websites about building connection and intimacy during sex often focus on what behaviours to do differently to build connection (More kissing! More eye contact! Slower penetration!) but stop short of explaining what these activities are accomplishing or how.

Feelings for One Another During Optimal Sexual Experiences

Many individuals distinguished between the feelings they had for their partners overall, and the feelings they experienced during magnificent sex that served to enhance the experience as it occurred – feelings of trust, safety, comfort, liking, acceptance, caring, closeness, intimacy and ease. As one woman put it: "And for me it wasn't so much about what we did necessarily, it was, I guess, the feelings, the connection, the togetherness, the enjoyment." Again and again, in various permutations, participants emphasized the marginal contributions of physical acts to great sex in favour of a broader perspective on magnificent sex.

Extraordinary lovers often talked about the importance of caring and closeness when talking about the dénouement of sex, the afterplay. Many said that after optimal sexual experiences, they do not roll over and go to sleep but instead cuddle, connect and bond with their partners. As one person put it, "Not doing anything and being close." Another woman said, "When we're finished making love I feel happy to be with him" (contrast this description with Billy Crystal's look of post-coital dread in *When Harry Met Sally*). Those we interviewed talked about how important it was for them to feel special to their partners and feel desired during sex. They emphasized the importance of feeling cared for in the moment and how that served to support an overall feeling of being cared for within the relationship. An older woman described one of the three greatest sexual experiences of her life, which involved multiple partners simultaneously: "The men really, really liked me. Yeah, they really, *really*, really liked me, and I knew it. I mean just the way they treated me, so wonderful. Like I felt like dessert."

Extraordinary lovers talked about feeling genuinely accepted and safe during the encounter, which was for many, a transformative experience. One person said, "There's a sense of, sort of, just sort of sinking into a safe comfortable place with the other person." One man described different kinds of trust: "There's the trust that in that sexual situation, you won't be raped or hurt, and you can be vulnerable with that person in that little space of time." Trust was important not only on its own but also because it could facilitate so many other contributors that helped to bring about or enhance a sexual experience in progress. Feelings of acceptance and safety were strongly connected to other important in-the-moment contributors like letting go, being authentic and feeling immersed. For example:

> Um, there's a sense of acceptance that, you know, whatever comes up that there's room for that and if we're in the middle of something and there's fear, there's room for that, and if we're in the middle of something and the fantasy shifts a little bit, there's room for that. Um, if we're in the middle of, of great sex and, you know, we need to leave, or somebody's penis has gotten soft, or, or whatever, whatever is there we can work into it and it's not the end of anything.

Participants talked about feeling really comfortable and relaxed together. One man talked about the importance of feeling "emotionally entwined" with his lovers:

> Feeling like, um, there is nothing she is holding back from me that if she told me, I would run away. Or there is nothing I am holding back from her that if I told her, she would become defensively aggressive.

Trust is often highlighted as an important aspect of successful relationships, and even of sexual relationships, but the active role that it plays *during* a sexual encounter seems to come up less often. (In general, the links between the overall qualities of a relationship and how those qualities play out in the bedroom have not been addressed often by sex researchers.) While trust might seem on the surface to be a more mundane contributor, it is actually a factor that might allow for sex to be exciting, spontaneous, wild and awesome. Reciprocally, the experiences of letting loose and being authentic with another person can serve to reinforce an overall sense of trust and safety in the relationship, and increase the future likelihood of magnificent encounters.

Light-Heartedness and Freedom

Working to build a light-hearted atmosphere together enhanced extraordinary lovers' feelings of ease and comfort, and the more comfortable and at ease they felt with one another, the more they could relax, play and laugh. One man described the connection between humour, comfort and intimacy within his relationships:

> I often over-simplify it by saying that, that uh, um, I'm really in favour of relationships where it's possible to laugh in bed [laughs]. And, um, it takes a certain level of comfort for most people to, to be kind of at ease with what's going on sexually and, and to have, to be able to simply laugh when something is absurd and it's really that comfort and intimacy that I think a lot of times uh, makes for great sex.

A woman explained why it was important for good lovers to know how to laugh, "So that if things don't go as expected, whatever that means, that no one feels devastated or no one feels that it's the reflection on their personhood but that it's just the way the rest of life is."

Extraordinary lovers said that it was easier to be spontaneous, creative and joyful in at atmosphere that was light-hearted and playful. This also enhanced the possibilities for bringing imagination and creativity into optimal sexual experiences. One woman explained:

> I think it um, my partner and I both have very creative imaginations and we have so much fun, um, playing out fantasies or coming up with different ways to, to tweak each other and to, um, just set each other, kind to set each other up.

Part of what makes sexual encounters magnificent in the moment for many is feeling unselfconscious, unrestrained, able to let go and be uninhibited. As one man said, "Her whole body is mine and my whole body is hers." Spontaneity, flexibility, adaptability and improvisation helped to create a sense of total sexual freedom or as described by several people, "No holds barred." Although we had originally asked questions about specific activities or sex acts (e.g., intercourse), they became increasingly absurd as one person after another told us that the actual acts were irrelevant. Hardly anyone cited a particular behaviour as a "must-have" for an optimal sexual experience. Rather, they focused on the potential for magnificent sex to embody exploration, freedom and flexibility. A male sex therapist described his definition of freedom:

> That doesn't necessarily, necessarily mean sort of swinging from the chandeliers, it's just that there'd be a freedom of movement that you wouldn't wonder how would the other view this or think this. It would be an automatic trust that they would like it.

Similarly, a woman talked about the novelty and freshness that she and her partners brought to magnificent sex, and characterized this as "the sense of discovery and wonder" that helped her to bring about optimal sexual experiences.

To be clear, although participants did talk about how light-heartedness could enhance an experience, no one suggested that the entire sexual encounter would be non-stop laughter. Rather, the tone of the encounter could shift from moment to moment and contain multiple layers. Sex could be hot and erotic and connected and intimate and light-hearted, at the same time or one after the other. Freedom and flexibility worked in concert to build an optimal sexual experience. This is another contributor that works its magic directly to create magnificent sex and also indirectly through its effects on other important elements.

11
THE META-FACTOR
Empathic Communication

One of the major ideas that arose repeatedly as we explored magnificent sex was the importance of communication. It was cited as a skill; as a characteristic of the relationships in which magnificent sex might occur; as something lovers might do beforehand to prepare for sex, during an optimal sexual experience or afterwards to debrief and lay the groundwork for future encounters. Communication came up when participants talked about changes, growth and development across their lives.

Sexual communication has commonly been equated with sexual self-disclosure, which is usually understood as a willingness to share one's sexual history with a partner, particularly in relation to the risk of sexually transmitted infections or to disclosing preferences for certain sexual behaviours or techniques. Scales measuring sexual communication include items like, "How much have you told your partner about the way you like to be touched sexually?" To a more superficial extent, the media tend to advocate significant restrictions on what information can be communicated, when this can be done and how (with great care to avoid the potential for hurt feelings), advising caution to engage in communication during "neutral times" so as not to generate anxiety (e.g., while eating dinner but not right after sex).

By contrast, extraordinary lovers use the word "communication" in the broadest sense, to include the possibility of sharing every aspect of their sexual and non-sexual selves by giving and receiving verbally and via touch. Communication emerges as an altogether more complex phenomenon than has been understood traditionally in literature or in popular definitions. Those we spoke to talked about reading their partners' verbal and non-verbal communications, responding to subtle cues and making ongoing modifications so as to enhance their sexual encounters. Or we could just go with the definition of communication offered by one woman we interviewed:

> It's the ability to go 'Hi! I find you remarkably attractive' or some variant thereof. 'You look like dessert, I'd like to see how you taste.' Or 'I'd like to see how you look dressed up in screams and leather.'

Empathic Communication as a Crucial Link

Communication helps couples to develop and express deep levels of empathy and to create an atmosphere conducive to optimal sexual experiences. Communication is fundamental in facilitating exploration, experimentation and discovery. Going on sexual adventures with another person requires extensive verbal and non-verbal communication. It can help strengthen the connection between partners and deepen intimacy.

More importantly, touch can be used as a vehicle for communication. At the most fundamental level, these kinds of empathic communications entail literally and figuratively feeling and allowing ourselves to be felt and known deeply and penetrated metaphorically as individuals and as erotic beings via touch itself. This extends beyond sharing of information to sharing of the self via touch.

Communication: The Basics and Beyond

As one person explained, communication could "be verbal, it can be vocal sounds that are not words, it can be nonverbal cues, something very overt like picking up a hand and putting it someplace else." Some regarded sexual encounters per se as potentially advanced forms of communication. A female sex therapist stated, "If one thinks of sexual intercourse as the apex of all intercourse, of social intercourse, that sexual relationship becomes the epitome of the best kind of communication we have between partners." One woman described kissing:

> It's just a very strong place to communicate and I think that's why many of the people that I talk to over the years who have had low desire or low frequency in fact do not kiss or have stopped kissing.

A man described this type of non-verbal responsiveness using a musical analogy:

> It's a sense that somehow you're in the same groove, like the best jazz combo, and that expresses different ways with different people. Sometimes it's through the eyes, sometimes it's in the hands, sometimes it's mostly through the genitals, but it's usually in the eyes, in the hands, and in the contact improvisation of the whole thing.

For extraordinary lovers, communication about sex is woven into the fabric of their daily lives and conversation. The content of communication might include likes, dislikes, preferences, interests, desires, fantasies, memories, plans and other intimate details. Communication might be used to discuss sex in general or to plan specific erotic encounters. Extraordinary lovers described the importance of clarity, specificity and precision in communication. One woman remarked:

> The ability to be vulnerable with a person is, I think, a *key* ingredient. And I don't mean vulnerable as in like being able to, to break down and share one's deepest secrets with the other person but more like the ability to share . . . real-ness of yourself. So real feelings, really what's going on and not, not have to go through the dance of communication that you have to in so many other times. Being able to feel comfortable and really say what you need or what you're getting, and all of that.

Extraordinary lovers said that they used communication to push their own comfort levels and to reveal themselves more completely to their partners. One man talked about the joy he was currently experiencing through communication: "The great thing about having a partner now where I feel comfortable is to be able to reveal that like, you know, I like to be very sadistic or, and / or I like to be very masochistic." Several described the joy of revealing themselves in this way.

Although many people assume that communication and spontaneity are antithetical (e.g., "too much talking kills the mood"), extensive communication can actually facilitate sexual spontaneity. Preparation and extensive communication allowed for improvisation during sexual encounters and within relationships. For example:

> If I say for myself, it doesn't really come down to just happenstance, it's a very purposeful and deliberate act. And if I want to have great sex, then I've got to be willing to notice and communicate.

In some cases, talking itself led directly to magnificent sex:

> Another thing that leads to great sex is . . . real emotional communication. I mean some, some wonderful things have happened between us where there's been some pain or grief on the table, and we've finally gotten to a place where, you know we'd be sitting really close, and just weeping and hugging and talking and sharing it and working it out. And then that gradually morphs into actual erotic territory. And that's that gentle, that sweet healing sex is also fabulous and great.

Communication During and After Sexual Encounters

During sex, some preferred brief and targeted exchanges. As one man put it, "succinct and to-the-point verbal communication which doesn't take too long to figure out or talk ourselves out of the mood." Others preferred more extensive conversation:

> I like lots of time, lots of connection, lots of communication. Usually I like interspersed periods of sex with interspersed periods of, with periods of just, you know, hanging out and talking and eating.

Communication during sex allowed for feedback and adjustment, to understand what their partners were thinking and feeling and try to meet one another's needs. One woman described how she went about doing this:

> I've always just done a lot of asking: 'Does this feel good? Does that feel good?' You know, and kind of just tailoring whatever I'm doing to them. 'Do you like my legs up here? Do you like them down there?'

Another person explained: "I think you need to ask, you know, 'Do you like that or do you not like that?' or, 'Do you like that *tonight* or do you not?'"

Communication helped extraordinary lovers to bring intentionality to the sexual encounter and to create and heighten eroticism.

Similarly, checking in or "talking about it afterwards" and debriefing were considered very important by many of those we interviewed. One man explained the purpose of these conversations:

> And we regularly, sort of after sex will reconnect and talk about you know, what worked and what didn't work and what were

you thinking when I did that and did I read that correctly so that we can kind of figure each other out. And there can be more of spontaneously doing what works instead of spontaneously doing something that ruins the mood or something like that.

Receiving Communication

Being sensitive, responsive, empathic and really aware of one's partner were fundamental skills. There was a real emphasis on the ability to read and respond accurately to a partner, listening carefully and paying close attention. One man explained:

> I've never really had sex with a partner who didn't pay attention to me in some way. But, I suppose that if I had sex with someone who was so intent on, just, whatever, doing whatever that they need to do or they want to do to me, and wasn't paying attention to my breathing, or what I'm saying or how I'm moving, that would be bad sex.

One woman believed that her ability to read and respond to her partners was her most valuable skill:

> Well I think that the best skill a lover can have is, like I said, taking direction well [laughs] and being responsive and observant. I mean so much I know of what I feel and what I've heard from partners makes me a good partner is that I'm able to see by breathing or how their body is flushing or muscle tension or whatever, I can sort of read a person.

That is, if you're paying attention to your partner's words and bodily responses in the moment, that is the primary skill you will need to create magnificent sex. Another woman said:

> People I think who are great in bed seem to have a, an almost uncanny ability not only to hear what's said but what isn't said. One time I told my current partner, 'You know, you're doing just what I wanted' and she said, 'Well, I'm watching your reactions.'

An older woman explained, "Let your partner know that you're enjoying him and having a good time and what he's doing is right." Receiving feedback while in the midst of a magnificent sexual encounter was critical for redirections and ensuring that the encounter was optimal for everyone. One woman provided a helpful illustration of paying attention:

> Um, [my partner] has some nerve damage down his left side. And I noticed fairly early in the relationship how, if I would run my fingers down his arm, he would hold his breath. And, and from one second to the next, he would either gasp or, or his eyes would close or something, some little sign that something there was happening and it was because, because of the nerve damage he can feel my hand and then not feel it and then feel my hand, and so that's become, kind of a fun thing to do because he never knows when he's going to feel that touch. It's paying attention to little things. Little things that, that get a reaction or don't get a reaction or get a negative reaction . . .

Another woman described her close attention to her partners' bodies: "I'm looking for where they have freckles, where they have scars."

Many emphasized how much their partners' communication enhanced their own personal excitement and arousal. They told us how they took great joy in being on the receiving end of open and authentic communication from their partners. They described the exquisite pleasure of having partners reveal something intimate about themselves. One woman said:

> I really like it when I'm having sex with somebody and they reveal what they really like, which is hard for people to do, you know? . . . I mean, that's a rush for somebody to actually reveal that and to have it accepted and then 'Wow! Let's play with this.'

Empathic Communication Can Grow with Experience

For many extraordinary lovers, the importance of communication grew stronger over time. Almost everyone we interviewed found that moving towards magnificent sex involved learning more and better communication strategies. Most did not learn how to communicate about sex while they were young. In fact, many of them were told specifically *not* to talk about sex (because it's dirty). So overcoming early life lessons was sometimes quite a challenge. For many, finding the words to articulate the deepest, darkest, most authentic parts of their selves opened doors to unimagined realms. One person explained how discovering the leather community improved understanding of communication:

> Um, and being able to talk about it openly, it's a community of folks that, um where I find in general, there's a focus on really clear and open communication, um, communication without shame, the ability to talk about your desires, um, is so much more mainstream than even expected or required. Um that I had to begin thinking about those things and sort of exploring in my own mind 'Well what do I actually like?' and 'What do I actually want more of?' and 'What would I like to try more of?' and 'How can I communicate those things?' and, you know, here's someone who's told me very clearly, 'If you don't like what I'm doing, let's think about how it could be better', and being asked those questions that challenged to think of sex as something that I can talk about and work on and mold and really get my hands dirty and love it as a full experience in the same way that these folks were doing with SM, um, was I think what made the difference for me.

One man described the long journey he had taken to develop his communication skills:

> And one of the things that has come, become very clear to me but never came into practice until relatively recently because I found it difficult, and that was being able to talk. Not just before and after, but during. Being able to say 'That feels good', or 'More of that please', or 'I'd rather not do that right now', or 'How would you feel about', or whatever . . . I think the biggest the biggest ingredient that I would say has presented itself through work – not just naturally but through pushing it – is communication and I, I think that communication and honesty – because communication isn't always honest – but communication and honesty, uh, to me are, are the most cherished, um, incendiary ingredients to great sex.

Similarly, an older man told us, "I've learned more to communicate, I guess is what I would say [chuckles] . . . learn much more to be able to just ask for what I want, and much more open to what is wanted."

In many cases, participants learned communication strategies from their partners; in other cases, formal learning through reading, attending workshops or interacting with a sex-positive community was helpful. Developing communication skills helped extraordinary lovers to find their voices, allowing them to communicate better in their everyday lives and to be more expressive with partners during sex.

Optimal Erotic Intimacy as Empathic Communication in Motion

Another woman struggled to define what she meant by empathy and decided to try a descriptive approach:

> Let me talk about my husband. He has a particularly wonderful way of touching another human being. Doesn't matter if it's just for caring or making contact or whether it's sexually, there's just something that he knows, or that he has in his body that he *does*, which is just, uh, right, um, and, and not, um, not jerky, not uncomfortable, not awkward.

These lovers were able to read their partners' communications and respond to subtle non-verbal cues. One woman described her personal experience of attentiveness and responsiveness from a partner:

> You know, it's funny: I could liken this to – and this is just a bizarre thing but bear with me – it's sort of like when you're a baby and you don't have to say anything and your mother or caretaker, whoever just knows what to do to make you feel better. And a really good sex partner is like that [laughing]! So it's like this wonderful, visceral, there's like this depth there. It's primitive. It's deep.

We will need to reconsider a myriad of ideas and concepts related to sexuality. At heightened levels of empathy, partners could help one another to delve deeply and express feelings beyond what each was initially capable of on their own; there is power in staying present and engaged with one another during moments of deep self-exploration. This level of empathy enhanced couples' intimacy, promoted respect and consideration towards one another, helped them to establish a safe, comfortable and trusting environment to venture further and ultimately facilitated the process of learning, development and exploration together. When it comes to magnificent sex, empathy is the linchpin of relational qualities.

12

THE PATHWAYS TOWARDS MAGNIFICENT SEX

What is the route to magnificent sex? It is now time to begin connecting the dots from the interviews to examine how the elements weave together to create optimal erotic experience as well as to hint at the implications for couples (which will be the focus of the final chapter). In this chapter, we introduce some of the patterns and sequences of elements which combine to produce magnificent sex. We have described the components of magnificent sex and the factors which facilitate its occurrence. But how do extraordinary lovers get there? Is there a pathway? More specifically, is there one, correct pathway?

We ask these questions because the field of sex and couples therapy has been divided about the "right" way for the last 20 years or so. There are at least a couple of points of view on the required foundations to move towards fulfilling sexuality in relationships. Is it the personal qualities of the individuals or is it the nature of their relationship itself which is most critical in shaping their sex lives? One perspective, based in family systems theory (Bowen, 1978), emphasizes the role of emotional maturity or "differentiation" (Schnarch, 1991, 2009). Proponents argue that individuals must be capable of standing on their own two feet and holding their own, particularly in conflict, so as to enable them to share their erotic desires without needing – surely wanting but not needing – another's affirmation that they and their wishes are acceptable (Schnarch, 1991, 2009). It takes a strong individual to maintain and assert one's sense of self as "good enough" regardless of what others might think. However, it is precisely that maturity that is required if one is to pursue one's heart's desires in the face of others, particularly loved ones, who may look askance at such wishes.

Another point of view is rooted in attachment theory (Bowlby, 1969) and emphasizes relationships that nourish a sense of safety (Johnson, 2004). The connection between two people in a committed relationship creates the bedrock in which even those with chaotic upbringings, who were insecure in childhood, can grow personally and interpersonally. It is this emotional context that must be fostered in order to enable sexual fulfillment. By contrast, it is damage to the interpersonal bond, for example, by clandestine infidelity, which can tear at the fabric of a sexual relationship.

There are still others who argue that intimacy is the enemy of the erotic (Perel, 2006). Domestic intimacy, in particular, is regarded from this vantage point as an oxymoron; from this perspective, the entire notion that one can find domestic bliss (e.g., maintain a home, raise children) in the same relationship that is also to provide the fodder for erotic desire is a historical anomaly. It is asking for too much. A certain amount of separateness rather than interdependence is required to bring eroticism home.

Who among these therapists has it right? What do our data on optimal erotic intimacy gleaned by studying extraordinary lovers reveal about the foundations and pathways towards magnificent sex? The data reveal that each of these approaches are correct, though not necessarily for all clients and not necessarily in the same sequence for each individual in their relationships. From the peak of the mountain, the view is always superb; however, the pathways to the mountaintop are hardly uniform – they are unique.

The Pathways: Is It Attachment or Differentiation? Yes!

For some extraordinary lovers, it was the nature of their relationship that allowed for the emergence of individual qualities, which then led to magnificent sex. We refer to this as Pathway A. However, in other instances, the sequence was precisely reversed: In these cases, Pathway B, the qualities of the individual had a markedly positive impact on the development of the relationship which, in turn, contributed to optimal sexual experiences.

Pathway A: Relationships that Facilitate an Individual's Way of Being

Specifically, for many extraordinary lovers, the characteristics of the relationship gave rise to the kinds of personal qualities which led to magnificent sex. For example, a relational atmosphere of trust, safety, intimacy and love might allow individuals to let go of and heal from negative messages heard or even trauma experienced during childhood or adolescence. Some individuals mentioned the effects of trust and safety as enabling the erotic abandon which is characteristic of magnificent sex. This was illustrated by a rather succinct comment: "You have to feel safe enough to be wild." Another woman described the impact upon her after a special moment intensified the couple's trust:

> So we went back to his, his, uh, we went back to the hotel room and we had the best sex we've – he made me oink like a pig [laughter], you know what I mean? And it was really kind of just a breakthrough because, um, I felt like I could be as nasty and as, and as crazy as I wanted to be because I trusted him. For some reason, our trust level had deepened in that, in that dinner.

Trust in the relationship and in the partner made it safe to be authentic which then led to the capacity to explore or to be swept away as suggested by a participant who said:

> I guess the commonality in the relationship is the, um, but the trust and the mutual respect . . . and that would be, you know, in order to have that ability to be that vulnerable and the ability to give up that control that I have that trust.

We were especially moved by the comments from some of the older individuals who described how this pathway might emerge in long-term relationships:

> I have several friends who have been married for thirty, forty, fifty, one of them married sixty years and um, they have fabulous sex, they said that sex is better than it's ever been, because their connection with each other is so deep and so strong that there's no anxiety about rejection or inhibitions. They just can really let go and let loose and be intimately connected in a sweetness that they tell me they've not had before their seventies. And one of them's in their eighties.

Or as a woman described:

> I have to say that the best sex of my life is happening now with my husband after we've worked through certain problems and actually came clean about what we really want and what's really motivating us sexually. And I think given that trust, um, given that

communication has created a situation where we can really play, and kind of push limits and try new things and it's been, it's been great.

This kind of relationship built on joint effort, the willingness to confront relational challenges, open sexual communication and trust hardly seems to suffer from the damper of domestication. On the contrary, it has led to the conditions in which this couple is free to "push limits" in bed, thereby developing erotic intimacy.

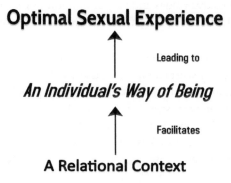

Optimal Sexual Experience

Leading to

An Individual's Way of Being

Facilitates

A Relational Context

Pathway A: Relationships that Facilitate an Individual's Way of Being

There are numerous other combinations of relational qualities which engender individual development, which then results in magnificent sex. Another example involves a connection characterized by acceptance and support which leads to greater authenticity, growth and comfort with oneself which in turn makes for delightful sex. As a woman commented, "So I think a kind of playful connection, uh, helps the, you know, being able to feel accepted by the other person helps, really accepting yourself sexually, uh, is another piece of it." As another said:

> What's happened now is, um, you know, through accepting and through the fact that I'm, you know, I think [my husband's] amazingly sexy and I tell him that all the time. He's just like 'Oh my God, the way you think of me it's, you know [laughing], it's not true' but I think that has kind of helped give him a bit of that fantasy that he wanted, you know, of being secure in his sexuality . . . I think, it's the acceptance that I gave him, the fact that I was willing to work through the problems with him, um, and he's got a heck of a lot more confidence in his own sexuality now.

Pathway B: Individual Qualities that Facilitate a Relational Quality

By contrast, sometimes it is the personal qualities of one (or both/all) of the individual(s) in a relationship which create the conditions for people to thrive, thereby creating the pathway towards optimal sexual experiences. For example, an individual who believes that sexuality takes effort in a long-term relationship may lead to the couple valuing and prioritizing sexual relations, which can create the foundations for magnificent sex. Similarly, an individual with strong, sex-positive values and lack of inhibitions can rub off on the partner(s), who can then let loose together in their sexual relations:

> I think being positive about it is a good thing and I enjoy it and I don't make any secret about it. You know, I don't pretend I don't do it and I don't pretend I don't like it. So, uh, people, people have often found me very sexy just because I'm not afraid of it. And because I do like it and I think because I'm pretty relaxed and comfortable about that, it makes the other person much more relaxed and comfortable about it.

Or, as another participant described herself:

> I think that's one of the beauties of, of having sex with me is because I always let go so much that I think it, it kind of gave permission to, to people to be more uninhibited, to make more noise, you know, 'cause they've got this girl who's just like 'Woo hoo!!', you know, throwing off the clothes and jumping in and diving right in, um, and I think that's why I've probably had a lot of great sex. It's 'cause I kind of [laughing] carried my partners along with me.

In other instances, it was an individual's curiosity, sexual openness and interest in the unexpected which led to exploration within the relationship, which led to magnificent sex. In still other cases, it was one person's willingness and skill in talking about sex candidly which enabled deeper, more extensive communication in the relationship. One can imagine almost any of the individual qualities of extraordinary lovers facilitating the relational characteristics which then lead to magnificent sex.

Pathway B: Individual Qualities that Facilitate a Relational Quality

Occasionally, we encountered individuals who valued especially inde-
pendent partners: For example, one man explained, "Knowing that my
partners were able to take care of themselves" enabled him to "ride
the experience and not have to worry." Similarly, another participant
commented:

> Yeah. Um, one of the characteristics that I think is very impor-
> tant for me is that I need to be – I need to feel like the partner
> is very competent and capable of taking care of themselves.
> I don't, when I feel like I have to take care of the partner and
> worry if they're going to be like, okay afterwards or if some-
> thing I'm going to do is going to *bother* them or *upset* them,
> then that either results in me just not entering into sex at all or
> being very sort of cautious about it and that tends not to result
> in great sex. Whereas if I'm with a partner that I feel that even
> if something goes *wrong* or something is *upsetting* or, you know,
> there's even a worst case scenario that it will be fine and we'll
> talk it over and we'll keep going, then that tends to result in me
> feeling more free to be spontaneous and do whatever I feel good
> and that tends to result in great sex. So a partner who has that
> quality is very important to me.

These comments are a clear expression of the need, at least by some individuals, of having or being/becoming the kinds of partners who are capable

of the maturity and self-soothing (Schnarch, 1991) which enables both people to be freer as they move towards erotic intimacy.

Pathways A and B Intertwining?

Sometimes, participants suggested that extraordinary lovers seek out those who are their match. Especially for the older individuals, experience had taught them not to settle for partners who were not their psychological and erotic equals. As these people described what they sought in order to maximize the opportunities for magnificent sex, their comments suggested that it wasn't differentiation or attachment that leads to optimal erotic experience but both intertwined:

> I think they probably look for those partners that they, you know, where they're attracted to the kind of people who will be able to provide that kind of, um, experience for them. So I think they'll be attracted to those same qualities in somebody and that will allow them the ability to have great sex. I think it's all, it's all circular.

This comment is reminiscent of Maslow's description of how individuals at the peak of human development select their lovers. Recognizing that most people end up in relationships with people who might be well-suited to them in, for example, appearance but not intellect or personality or vice versa, he contrasted the choices of the average person with those who are most integrated (1970, p. 202):

> The people with whom [self-actualizers] fall in love are soundly selected by *either* cognitive or conative [meaning behavioural] criteria. That is, they are *intuitively, sexually, impulsively* attracted to people who are right for them by cold, intellectual, clinical calculation. Their appetites agree with their judgments, and are synergic rather than antagonistic. [emphasis in the original]

Maslow's findings more than 50 years ago from his research on the higher reaches of human potential are consistent with the findings from our studies and the wisdom of extraordinary lovers. Thus, with emotional maturity, individuals seek out just the right people to be their own, special partners, thereby creating relationships in which each person and their relationships can be fulfilled and continue to grow. This encapsulates the intersection of the differentiation/attachment debate. We do not need to focus on one to the exclusion of the other; rather, we can mature and grow with another person, and use that bond to foster our own development. We can build both at the same time. As one sex therapist put it: "It gets better as you get older if you're smart enough to grow into your capacity for being human."

Pathway C: Affirming One's Own Value and the Right to Pleasure

Pathways A and B were the most predominant routes to magnificent sex. However, there were some individuals for whom there were other routes to optimal sexual experience. For some, the pathway towards optimal sexual experiences involved their relationships with themselves. One woman captured this saying:

> I think great sex involves a certain amount also of, how can I put this, um, finding oneself attractive and I think, um, from a woman's perspective anyway, sometimes I think that's almost more important than finding the other person attractive or that they find you attractive is that, um, when you're having great sex, um, I think you're very turned on and connected to your partner but you're also very turned on and connected to yourself.

Another participant underlined the importance of a sense of a self that includes the belief that one is worthy of sexual pleasure:

> If we can believe that sex is our entitlement, that good sex, great sex is our entitlement and that there's nothing wrong with enjoying our bodies and that turning on the lights is a good idea and making noise is also a good idea and being expressive and adventuresome and trying something new, um, would just be a terrific thing, to, to do tonight, then good sex happens and, um, and, and we enjoy it. If we, if we don't be in our own way then sex gets better and better.

These sentiments might be thought-provoking for those who hardly think it appropriate to raise our young to anticipate sexual delight. Too few children and teens are encouraged to see fulfilling sex as an "entitlement". On the contrary, most youth and young adults are subject to the kind of sex education that focuses on the dangers of sex; self-respect is to come from abstention (Lamb, Lustig & Graling, 2013). The consequences of such "educational" approaches will arise in our chapters on the clinical implications of our research, just ahead. As another participant summarized, "It's like we swim through great sex from birth to death and it's just our ability to embrace it that determines whether we experience it."

Pathway D: Erotic Preferences

For a minority of participants, what was essential to make sex magnificent was related to their particular erotic preferences. Sometimes these were esoteric and in other instances they might be perceived as mundane. Most individuals did not identify any particular sexual act as necessary for optimal sexual experiences but the few who did usually mentioned kissing. For example, "There is something about kissing and the intimacy of kissing, the passionate kissing that . . . that kind of creates a certain kind of arousal and connection." Others had a predilection for combining particular activities:

> You alternate flogging the back . . . and kissing and stroking so it becomes very sweet and pleasurable . . . back and forth, and up and down, however you want to look at it, um, you know, a rapid pace and a slow pace. Kissing, a sucking, a licking, breathing on, a light touch and a heavy touch, all these kinds of varieties overload the body with incredible sensations that are part of the portal of great sex, of attaining, of having a great experience.

A man explained the role of intercourse in his sexual relations as follows: "That's how physically we can join to one another. It's a *beautiful* thing to be able to join physically with another body. To actually take a part of my body and insert it in hers and to have it be pleasurable for her . . . So it is the ultimate."

Conclusion of Contributors to Magnificent Sex: Onwards Towards Desire

The facilitating factors described throughout Part III are not a checklist of requirements; they are intended to provide specific examples of the contributions of various elements to magnificent sex. They are extensive enough – encompassing particulars of development from childhood to old age, of preparation, of individual and relationship qualities in general and how they play out during optimal sexual experiences, of skills and most especially, empathic communication – that readers may wonder, "What does it matter?" These contributors have particular implications for dealing with sexual problems. And therapists will need to remember that clients will define different factors as critical dimensions and pathways towards improved or perhaps even optimal sexual experiences.

Therapists are called upon to support clients as they struggle with substantive personal growth and relational depth. Although both are essential, some clients will be inclined to focus on one path while other clients may emphasize a different route to the same peaks. While clinicians aim for empirically-based approaches, we will also need to customize the focus of therapy to the needs of particular clients/couples (i.e., individual, relational, contextual). If we are to help couples to enhance their sex lives, we will need to forget standardized protocols and manualized treatment for matters of this complexity.

We began this book by noting that the most pervasive presenting problem in the realm of sex therapy is related to sexual desire. What have we discovered that might prove valuable to individuals, couples and their therapists in dealing with desire problems? That will be the focus of Part IV, the payoff, if you will, for studying what makes for magnificent sex, what it looks like in reality according to those who have lived it and what helped extraordinary lovers to create optimal sexual experiences.

PART IV

PART IV

13

IMPLICATIONS AND APPLICATIONS FOR LOVERS AND THERAPISTS WHO ASPIRE HIGHER

We began our research by wondering what magnificent sex might look like and what we might learn by studying extraordinary lovers. We identified the eight components of optimal sexual experience, the lessons gleaned from extraordinary lovers and how these experts managed to make their way to the peaks of erotic intimacy. We have learned that magnificent sex is multidimensional, requires considerable effort and is deeply rewarding. What are the implications for individuals and lovers, for couples and sex and relationship therapy?

We began this book by noting that problems of low/no desire/frequency and sexual desire discrepancy are among the most common problems encountered in sex therapy (Charest & Kleinplatz, 2018; Kleinplatz, 2018). What have we learned from extraordinary lovers that could be helpful to these clients/ patients? This chapter will attempt to weave these threads together and contextualize desire problems by contrasting them with optimal erotic intimacy. We then introduce a new therapy approach developed by studying magnificent sex.

Individuals and couples who are distressed by low desire or sexual desire discrepancy typically have an unspoken belief system which includes the assumption that if they were normal, they would feel desire. People ought to want sex. It is only natural. But what kind of sex is it that one ought to want, with whom, in what context and under which circumstances?

What – If Anything – Do We Wish to Promote?

One of our concerns is about what we wish to promote through this work. In the years after our research team first began to disseminate our findings in conference presentations and publications, our colleagues would say that this is all very interesting, but given the complexity of the data, does it have any clinical utility? Does it have any application beyond the scholarly knowledge of what optimal sexual experiences look like among extraordinary lovers? Indeed, we too were wrestling with this interesting question which called for an empirical answer. We were warned by well-meaning colleagues that couples have it tough enough just trying to have any sex at all. Would the results of our research tell them that managing to have sex despite a mortgage, two jobs, three kids and constant, utter exhaustion is not good enough? Are we actually trying to raise the bar even higher?

We wish to reiterate that our findings can educate about what can be – and not *should* be – attained. They are about possibilities – not requirements. Our goal, if anything, is to stop adding to existing pressures. People need to stop beating themselves up for not wanting to have sex when they have so much on their plates – unless the sex itself is irresistible. We want to let them – to let you – know that it is exceedingly common and absolutely "normal" that people are often in no mood for sex.

Couples often enter therapy wondering if their sexual frequency is "normal" or "abnormal". Normal frequency is not the point, but the question illuminates part of the larger problem. The couple is trying to assess their sex life according to some externally imposed standard. No one can judge how often another person should be having sex and more importantly, only one individual can ever determine what quality of sex is worth getting all excited about – not the physician, not the marriage counsellor or sex therapist, not the partner or spouse, but only that particular individual.

If it is counterproductive to focus on meeting externally-imposed demands, it is correspondingly important and helpful to become centered enough to turn and look within to discover and ask for the kind of sex that makes you glow in the dark. Extraordinary lovers make it crystal clear that part of the secret of magnificent sex is knowing what they want and refusing to settle. That means *declining* to have sex unless and until that sex is desirable for the particular individuals in question.

Symptoms vs. Signposts?

By the time most couples distressed by sexual desire problems make their way to couples or sex therapists' offices, they have scanned the web, bought the magazines and manuals, tried the tips, tricks and techniques unsuccessfully and have become disillusioned. They have seen their physicians who have recognized that the poor couple is desperate and suggested that the parties split the difference: When one wants sex once a week and the other wants sex once a month, the physician often recommends that they compromise at once every second week. Not only does this suggestion prove ineffective but it backfires. The couple now has one more thing to quibble about and this time with greater resentment, though each has difficulty articulating why the problem now seems compounded. The physician's advice skirts the unspoken challenges underlying differences in desire and makes it harder to express the reasons for their disparity. The meanings of their reluctance to settle for this compromise are buried by the new arguments about the "every two week" prescription.

Part of the problem with the proposed solution originates in the conceptions of "sex"; extraordinary lovers explained that magnificent sex is not about genital friction and the ultimate end of sex need not be intercourse. Other problems originate in our limited definitions and conceptions of the nature and origins of the desire problem – or whatever the sexual problem, from erectile dysfunction to pain on penetration. From the inception of the field, the standard in conducting a comprehensive assessment of sexual problems entailed evaluating for intrapsychic, interpersonal, psychosocial and organic factors in the development and nature of sexual dysfunctions and disorders (Kaplan, 1974; Masters & Johnson, 1970). This multidimensional framework for conceptualizing sexual problems is well-taken. However, our findings suggest that we should consider another factor, that is, the quality of the sexual encounter. Is the quality of the sex satisfactory to each partner? Is the type of sex they engage in mutually fulfilling? Was it arousing? Was it intimate? Was it erotic? In short, was it sex worth wanting?

Sometimes people make assumptions based on the frequency of sex with disregard for the nature of the sex or sexual relationship that is wanted. To put it another way, is it any wonder if people who have different visions of ideal sexual relations ultimately appear to have a sexual desire discrepancy? Their visions need not be as glaring as one seeking BDSM while the other prefers vanilla or one seeking polyamory while the other dreams of monogamous intimacy for the rest of their lives. I [P.J.K.] recall working with a couple whose complaint was not spending enough time having sex. In fact, they had been complaining to one another for decades about why they didn't have more sex. It took surprisingly little time in conducting an assessment to ascertain that they each had different understandings of their problem and had discrepant visions of the perfect sex life. They both complained about "not enough sex" but one wanted a higher frequency of sexual relations while the other wanted to spend the whole day in bed every time they had sex. What was astonishing to me was that it took a visit to my office to clarify the nature of the problem.

Sometimes the link between low desire and sexual problems is more subtle. Rather frequently, patients are referred for treatment of the sexual dysfunctions (e.g., erectile dysfunction, difficulties with orgasm) rather than sexual desire disorders. However, the underlying "problem" is that they do not find the sex stimulating. Healthy individuals who engage in sex without desire on a regular basis will encounter difficulties with arousal. So that in a heterosexual couple, when his erection falters or her vagina becomes sore in mid-intercourse, it may be that they were (barely) aroused enough to begin intercourse but not sufficiently turned on to really enjoy it.

For example, each day women are referred for treatment by their gynecologists for pain on intercourse. The gynecologist has already examined her, found no obvious medical problem and has recommended applying a lubricant before "sex". Although the lube has diminished the pain upon penetration, she avoids sex even more than before. Her husband complains that before she gets around to having sex with him, the kids have to be fed, homework completed, in bed and asleep; lunches have to be ready for the next day, the house has to be cleaned, and so on. In other words, he feels lowest on her list of priorities. He feels rejected. She in turn, feels pressured to have sex whether or not she is "in the mood". But she notices – in fact, she is all too aware – that if she doesn't give in often enough, he'll get "grumpy" and she and the kids hate it when he gets "in a bad mood". So even though she feels no sexual desire, she actually initiates sex to prevent him from getting "grumpy". At first, he was touched by her reaching out to him. It meant something to him that she was clearly doing it for his sake. But the fact that she was disengaged during sex eventually led to his own reluctance to proceed. He wanted to be wanted – not accommodated merely to prevent turmoil. By the time they have been referred for therapy, they are having sex less than once a month and neither of them are enjoying it, whether or not they are having orgasms. What are we to make of this kind of common pattern, whether triggered by pain, erectile dysfunction or simply unfulfilling sex?

The alternative to "treating low desire" is to let people know that such symptoms are not necessarily indicative of dysfunctions so much as signposts saying, "Be careful. Pay attention. What is it that you really want? What changes do you need to make so that sex between you is worth wanting?" If you can tolerate waiting for sex until the conditions fill you with desire and arousal, your bodies will often take care of themselves . . . and when they don't, couples are often having too much fun to notice or care.

Promoting Erotic Intimacy

Helen Singer Kaplan (1974) suggested that while conducting a sexual assessment, clinicians ask clients to describe in vivid detail what takes place during their sexual relations, from the moment of initiation until they are both finished (whatever that might entail). The blow-by-blow description makes for a good beginning. However, therapists need more than what is observable to the fly on the wall or the video camera. Therapists also need to be able to imagine and feel what goes on in the minds and hearts of the individuals having sex, moment by moment.

Think back to the last time you had sex. Take a few moments and then please close your eyes until you can visualize and recall in vivid detail, using all your senses, how it felt, how your partner(s) felt to you, how you felt during the encounter and how you felt afterwards. How did it make you feel about the next time? For better and for worse, it's a simple sequence:

Memory→Sex→Anticipation/Dread→Sex→Memory→Sex→Anticipation/Dread→

Every time an individual engages in "sex", it leads to either heightening of anticipation or of dread for the next encounter. (Theoretically, it could leave one feeling neutral about the next time.) As an older man noted, "Memories [become] etched on your consciousness." As another articulated what might become the pivotal assessment question: "Do you think about it the next day and immediately get hot? How strongly did it etch itself on your mind and body?" As an older man indicated, when the sex is magnificent, "It creates anchor points – pleasure points which you can bring back." These lovers are talking about the kind of sex worth savouring, the kind that fills you with anticipation and delight just remembering it and looking forward to the next time. The shared accumulation of awesome memories adds to the unique intimacy in a relationship. An older individual reported, the shared memories are "reinforcing of the magic that we have." As an older, polyamorous man recounted:

> Every time that I'm with each one of them, part and parcel of what goes on during long, off-the-clock sex is historical discussion. And

reflection on where we've been, where we are, where we hope to be and with the acknowledgment that there's an awesome dynamic between and amongst the people involved.

There is a power in these kinds of experiences and the recollection of them that has a profound impact not only on the couple but on each individual, too. Optimal sexual experiences become self-perpetuating. An older woman said, "I am incredibly sexy and I know it."

On the other hand, if the last time you had sex it was mediocre, it will hardly inspire desire for the next time. If it was lousy, uncomfortable, painful or distant, lovers will not be seeking an encore. Couples seek therapist services, saying that sex for one (or both) has sunk to the bottom of their "to-do" lists. As therapists, our job is hardly time-management. Yet therapists are confronted with patients/clients who state that sex is no longer a priority. That may be an understandable response to the combination of real-life demands and uninspiring sex. We are not suggesting that the clinician's role is to talk patients/clients into caring about something that they genuinely find of no interest. However, how often is it the case that clients actually have no feelings about sex versus they are disillusioned but harbour faint hopes that someone can help nurture their dormant desires?

Sex and couples therapists can continue our attempts at alleviating dysfunction and pathology or we can aim for much grander outcomes indeed. As lovers, we can try to alleviate bad sex and get rid of the various obstacles to having sex at all or we can aim to create the kind of sex that automatically ranks higher on our list of priorities.

Re-Visioning Sex

What does this mean for couples and sex therapists in dealing with ordinary clients/patients? It means that we might aim higher than merely remediating symptoms of sexual problems (Charest & Kleinplatz, 2018; Kleinplatz, 2012). It may, however, require re-visioning sex itself. To the extent that all of us are defining sex as something commensurate with penetration, orgasm or reproduction, we are limiting ourselves to precisely the same, troubling, normative performance standards which generate sexual problems (Irvine, 2005; Reiss, 1991). Sometimes the therapist might consider freeing clients to re-envision sex – to pay attention to what makes them feel alive within while connected with each other during caressing and other sex play. This can be more advantageous than continuing on to whatever they define as the "sex act" without delight. If it doesn't feel great, stop. Alternately, it means helping clients to become so fully engaged with one another – not only at the level of physical stimulation but by encouraging them to continue exploring one another emotionally and erotically such that sex cannot help but be exciting.

The challenge for the therapist as well as for lovers entails contending with some of the paradoxes inherent in optimal sexual experiences. These include the challenge of being utterly embodied, absorbed and present within, while simultaneously being fully in synch with and connected with another person(s). Magnificent sex requires learning how to become and remain centered, while also letting go in erotic abandon in the moment.

The objective is not to suggest that all people ought to strive for extraordinary sexuality. Rather it is to acknowledge that those who have attained it had set out to do so and devoted substantial time, energy and development of interpersonal skills to make it happen. Extraordinary lovers practised the required skills even though this entailed making mistakes within view of their partners. They taught themselves to become more open, attentive and sensitive so that they could be absorbed with their partners in the moment. It is unlikely that optimal sexual intimacy will become a reality without notable efforts.

Attention to Individual Growth and Emotional Intimacy Are Essential for High Quality Sex

Sometimes, the qualities needed to create magnificent sex are so obvious that we can overlook and even neglect them. It is worth highlighting that cultivating both the intrapsychic and interpersonal dimensions are vital for creating optimal sexual experience. Each has a crucial role in creating and maintaining intense sexual connection. Among those we interviewed, individual maturity and self-knowledge helped to create an atmosphere of trust and trustworthiness. Correspondingly, trust was nurtured in an atmosphere of emotional accessibility and goodwill. The commitment to investing in the other's best interests is essential for the long-term development of the relationship. Mutual interest, knowledge and especially heightened empathy, expressed verbally and bodily, created the safety necessary to access and reveal deep vulnerabilities which in turn enabled intense, erotic exploration.

Extraordinary lovers argued with their partners at times about sex and other matters but they trusted each other enough to stay present even when they were uncomfortable, thus expanding their individual and shared comfort zones. They chose to communicate about their desires, even when they differed, with precision and transparency. In the face of struggles in their relationships, they chose to remain emotionally available even when that was scary, in the hope that the resulting vulnerability would be cherished as a gift. Extraordinary lovers talked about learning to take risks with their partners "in a safe way". Both partners became free to develop and mature over time without these changes being seen as threatening to the relationship.

Optimal erotic intimacy involves the abilities to be authentic within while engaged intimately with another and creating just enough emotional safety to allow for emotional exploration and risk-taking (Kleinplatz, 2016; Kleinplatz et al., 2018; Ménard et al., 2015). Keeping in mind the dual roles of personal independence and attachment, the goal of working with sexual desire problems in therapy is not to manage the problem but to make the space – and the relationship – *just safe enough* for the couple to take interpersonal and erotic risks together (Kleinplatz et al., in press).

The Risks of Erotic Intimacy versus the Risks of Erotic Stagnation

As our team has presented our findings and their implications over the last few years, our colleagues have asked repeatedly about what the dangers might be in what we are ostensibly promoting. They say that we are encouraging couples to go deeper into forbidden territory. They say there is a reason that couples are afraid to share their fantasies. Don't we realize, they ask, the emotional and interpersonal risks of too much erotic exploration?

They are right, of course, if what we are doing is telling couples how much to risk. We are very careful about what we promote. It is not the job or even the right of therapists to tell couples how much of their eroticism to reveal nakedly. However, correspondingly, as we help couples to weigh the pros and cons of their decision-making, we might consider the risks in aspiring towards optimal erotic intimacy alongside the risks inherent in erotic stagnation. It is that latter set of risks that rarely come to the fore but which may underlie a great deal of sexual boredom, frustration, alienation and loneliness.

Couples have an extraordinary amount of bad sex. One of the elements of bad sex that jumps out at me [P.J.K.] while seeing patients/clients all day long is silence. As my clients describe the minutiae – during assessments with all

present in my office – of their experiences of sexual "relations", I am struck
by the lack of any relating *during* sex in long-term couples, regardless of sex,
gender or sexual orientation of the individual and the partner(s). Each has
no clue as to what the other is thinking or feeling, let alone desiring, during
sex. My picture of them in bed is of silent cartoon characters with balloons
over their heads, talking to themselves rather than to each other while having
"sex", ostensibly "together".

Hook-ups, lovers, spouses . . . it's often crushingly lonely for the people
involved. Clients seem stunned when I reflect that impression aloud during
sex therapy sessions. And then they both nod and agree, each surprised then,
to discover that the other is agreeing, too. Each had no idea the other, also,
was lonely during sex.

A helpful, alternate perspective is generated by extraordinary lovers. Over
time and with experience, they had learned not to settle. As one older man
said, "I'm willing to make fewer compromises about what I want sexually as
I get older." Most people in dysfunctional or merely lacklustre sexual relationships with infrequent sex harbour this niggling fear about reaching a point of
desperation where they worry, "If I don't push for us to have sex, I/we will
never have sex again!!!" They share a belief that the higher desire partner is
like the Energizer bunny, *always* hopping about and hankering for more while
the lower desire partner *never* seems to want sex. The discrepancy between
them seems insurmountable. And that is precisely how the problem is main-
tained: The fact of two people being so polarized that they see each other as
diametrically opposed keeps them from ever having to take a close look at
other differences in their relationship. In addition, it stops them from examining the differences in their separate erotic wishes and preferences and visions
of sexual intimacy – let alone what conditions would make it worth their
while to get all excited together.

It is the anxiety about finally reaching a breaking point without sex –
where they will "cheat" or end the relationship or something bad – that
leads one to push and the other to settle for more sex, even though it is
not fulfilling sex. The problem is that each time one or both consents to
lousy sex, the greater the worry and outright reluctance for the next time.
(Please note that notwithstanding the impression that the low desire partner
is usually female and the high desire partner is usually male, this is not necessarily the case. Although the split is not quite down the middle, it is close.
In addition, there is plenty of sexual desire discrepancy in LGBTQ couples.
And please remember that there was no sex difference among extraordinary
lovers.)

The Sexual Relationship Death Spiral

There are 1,000 reasons as to why sex can be disappointing. The circumstances are extremely varied, broad and ubiquitous. Here are just a few:

- You have been having arguments that have yet to be resolved.
- Your partner has sexual fantasies that have never been shared. Your sex life does not resemble her fantasies.
- One or both of you have difficulty reaching orgasm during penetrative sex.
- You experience pain on penetration.
- Your partner experiences pain on penetration.
- One or both of you are sleep deprived.
- Your baby is crying. There is no money for child care.
- Your partner is turned off during your long, heavy periods.
- There is a history of brutal sexual abuse during your childhood which makes it hard for you to understand how anybody could possibly like "sex".
- Your partner has sleep apnea and the resulting chronic fatigue reduces sexual desire.
- Because each of you were unaccustomed to communicating openly, you read one another's physiological responses as evidence of "readiness" for "sex" instead of talking about your subjective levels of engagement and excitement.
- One or both of you have diseases or disabilities or use medications that affect sexual functioning.
- There has been a death in the family and you are each grieving in different ways.
- You are getting older and adapting to changes in body image.
- You are caring for older and/or sick family members, possibly at the same time that you are caring for children.

These are all good reasons for refraining from sexual activities until the underlying problem can be resolved or each of you re-vision sex in such a way, by mutual agreement and consent, that the obstacles can be dealt with successfully.

Unfortunately, that is not what most of the couples do most of the time. What they do instead is initially based in good intentions. Despite the lack of *sexual* desire, they proceed because of a commitment to the relationship. They know that sexual intimacy is important for the flourishing of a relationship. And so, with a measure of goodwill, one or both proceeds despite the lack of desire. When people enter into sex with this attitude, the sex will probably not be especially fulfilling. Partners might be able to get away with doing the other "a favour" every once in a while in a sexual relationship that is otherwise of very high calibre. When couples' sex lives begin to falter, if only out of a desire to maintain the vestiges of their sexual relationship, they begin to go through the motions of sex without really being engaged. They push themselves to participate in whatever "foreplay" necessary – or none at all – to demonstrate to one another that they have just had "sex" (Kleinplatz, 2011). It may or may not be barely passable. McCarthy and McCarthy (2020) say that in a good-enough sexual relationship, there will be occasional "duds". If these duds occur up to 15% of the time in an otherwise satisfying sexual relationship, they will not harm the overall quality of the couple's sex life. In fact, demonstrating goodwill via the occasional "favour" for one's partner in a long-term relationship demonstrates commitment and means the partner will probably reciprocate down the road. However, when people persist in having sex without *sexual* desire more often, the initial goodwill out of a sense of commitment becomes replaced by feelings of pressure from the partner and guilt from within. When these favours become habitual rather than rarities, problems will result from "just doing it" (Kleinplatz, 2011; Metz & McCarthy, 2012). So that whereas they initially chose to have sex out of commitment to relational harmony (i.e., having sex out of love or desire for intimate connection), they are now having sex without *sexual* desire more commonly.

If the partners now continue to have sex grudgingly, the unspoken goal from the lower desire partner will be to get the sexual event over with as quickly as possible in order to appease the higher desire partner. This means that the quality of their sexual interaction will decrease. There are now increasing episodes of mediocre sex. This means lowered arousal during sex and lower satisfaction after sex. It may take a while for the higher desire partner to realize that the low desire partner is not particularly engaged nor satisfied. For a time, the high desire partner has enjoyed their sexual activities sufficiently so that afterwards, he or she is eager for the next time; simultaneously, the lower desire partner is resentful that after his or her sacrifice in having sex for the sake of the relationship, he or she does not get the deserved break from having to even think about the next time. Nevertheless, they continue.

As the pattern progresses, the higher desire partner pursues sexually while the lower desire partner becomes increasingly and more conspicuously disengaged during sex. Thus, the quality of the sex continues to deteriorate becoming increasingly dread-full for the low desire partner and ultimately, for both. Sooner or later, if merely pleasing the partner or trying to avoid upsetting the partner becomes the predominant motive for having sex, the body will not lie. The signs and symptoms of what sex therapists will later diagnose as sexual dysfunctions begin to emerge: For example, during intercourse, his penis is just hard enough to penetrate his partner vaginally or anally but he is not aroused enough to sustain an erection or to have an orgasm. She is just wet enough to endure initial stimulation or penetration but not aroused enough for orgasm or sustained thrusting.

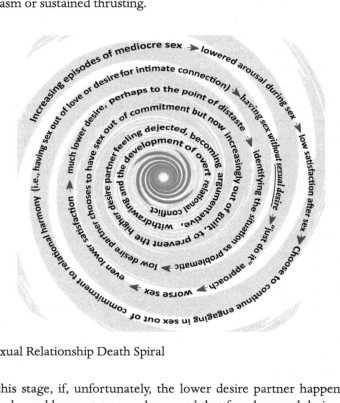

The Sexual Relationship Death Spiral

At this stage, if, unfortunately, the lower desire partner happens to be female, she and her partner may have read that female sexual desire may be more responsive rather than initiatory (Basson, 2001, 2002, 2005, 2010). (The notion in this 2001 model is that whereas men are capable of spontaneous desire – "ready, willing and able" – women are often more complicated.) If so, she may believe that she should "just do it" because if she simply throws herself into it, desire may emerge during sex, even though it was not there at the outset. If she is in a heterosexual relationship, and if the main course is intercourse, what if she really is beginning to feel aroused during intercourse? From the outside, she may look receptive (cf., Basson, 2001, 2002, 2005) and may even begin to get a bit aroused along the way. However, she may not have had time to really get off on it before "sex" is over. To the extent that we live in a society that equates sex with intercourse and further defines his ejaculation as the conclusion of sex, she may be left sexually frustrated once he ejaculates and they are done for the time being. At this point, she is entitled to become increasingly resentful and reluctant to engage in sexual activity entirely. However, by now, the higher desire partner is beginning to feel rejected and unwanted. To the extent that he or she now withdraws emotionally and becomes "grumpy" after too long without sex, the lower desire partner may concede and go along with the expectation of sexual compliance without any sexual desire, without goodwill, without much desire to foster intimacy, but merely with a desire to make the withdrawal and "grumpiness" cease. The low desire partner is now increasingly having sex out of guilt, to prevent the higher desire partner from feeling dejected, becoming argumentative and withdrawing and the development of overt relational conflict. At this point, the sex is of such poor quality that it's hard to imagine either one of them actually wants it. But by now, counting frequencies has become part of their arguments and the lower desire partner may actually initiate sexual activities if only to silently communicate, in essence, "So there! I've done it! Now leave me alone . . . You owe me that much." Canadians are fond of Olympic-calibre skating. We have come to call this the "Sexual Relationship Death Spiral" (as described in Charest & Kleinplatz, 2018; Kleinplatz, 2011, 2017).

The goal in these situations is to reverse the spiral and to replace dread with anticipation. But that requires changing the conversation from one focused on frequency to one focused on quality. When we asked extraordinary lovers about the consequences of extraordinary sex, they recounted wanting more. Correspondingly, when clients report, "If I never had sex again I wouldn't miss it", the sex in question wasn't spectacular. Or to put it another way, I have never heard anyone who had magnificent sex say, "If I never had sex again I wouldn't miss it."

But What of the Individual Who Says, "But I've Never Had Sexual Desire . . . No Fantasies . . ."?

"I never have *sexual fantasies*." Even this client will benefit from sensitive probing as to what will make it worthwhile to get all excited about being present and engaged during sex. Such individuals may not identify their fantasies as "sexual" in nature but as already discussed, our cultural definitions of sex tend to be so limited that many people will not even fathom the possibility that the fantasies they do have could be considered sexual. It may be surprisingly simple. It might require recollecting that day in grade six when they assigned your locker right next to that person you'd had a crush on. You couldn't believe how lucky you felt to have your locker so close to hers. You remember the way you felt butterflies in your stomach and bated breath when you saw her approaching and she said, "Hello." You felt your heart beating as you attempted to feign nonchalance and respond, "Hello." You spent the rest of the day floating. (You might be reminded of Charlie Brown's infatuation for / crush on 'the little red-haired girl' so hallowed to him that she never even needed a name in 50 years' worth of *Peanuts* comic strips.) You made an effort to run into her accidentally on purpose between classes all year long in hope of . . . well, *something* more. What that something might have looked like was not entirely clear. Clients may say that of course, they remember such moments but what do they have to do with sex?

The clinical challenge is to help identify sexual desire that isn't necessarily centred in the genitals. It's about those moments where one feels alive and wants *something* more. Yes, that was sexual desire – that is burgeoning sexual desire even though it was never named. This means that therapists will need to pose more sensitive inquiries as to the times when they have felt bodily tingling and delight at the thought of what might happen next. Clients are often surprised to hear that the moments when they feel excited inside and alive with anticipation are precisely the guideposts to greater sexual intimacy. It seems as though they have not even considered non-genital cues as relevant to enhancing the quality of sex.

And Then the Individual Adds, "If I Never Had Sex Again I Wouldn't Miss It . . ."

How are we to understand this remark? Please diagram this sentence. (For those readers who aren't old enough to have had a grade 4 teacher who was constantly requiring students to "diagram sentences", the term means to take the sentence apart, that is, into parts of the sentence or parts of speech.) In this case, we are about to dissect the sentence to see what meaning is embedded in each of the salient words. Let's begin with "If I never had *sex* again I wouldn't miss it . . ." In this case, the question becomes: What is the nature of the sex you wouldn't miss? Very likely, the nature and subjective quality of that sex leaves much to be desired. If you compared the best sex of your life to the sex you are so ready to forego, there is likely to be quite a difference between them.

Schnarch (1991) points out that in relationships in which sex has gone awry, it is the higher desire partner who initiates "sex" but it is the lower desire partner who initiates the shift to whatever act might draw the encounter to a close as soon as possible. For example, in heterosexual couples, it is typically the lower desire partner who will end "foreplay" quickly in order to engage in intercourse – usually the final act – so as to end that encounter. The irony is that in any couple with sexual desire discrepancy, it is the lower desire partner who is so eager to get it over with that he/she will rush towards the ultimate act – whatever that act might be for a given couple – so as make sex stop. It is interesting that over the last ten years or so, the term that individuals now use colloquially instead of the previous "orgasm" or "climax" is "finish". (For example, "Last night he had trouble finishing.") That choice of wording seems rather telling.

But the client adds: "And not only that . . . but *I've* never wanted sex . . ." The speaker is assuming that everyone should want sex. Sex is natural. It's a natural bodily function. Most of us are raised with the sorts of sex education that equate sexuality with reproduction. Our founders in the field of sex therapy, Masters and Johnson, too, equated sexual functioning with other bodily functions such as respiration, urination and defecation (Masters & Johnson, 1970, 1986). This conception of sexuality has remained embedded in our society and in the field. Consider whether this message that sex is natural is a sex-positive message or if perhaps it becomes the foundation for ignoring the context when one has minimal interest in sex. There is little "natural" about desirable sex. It is more akin to eating. It, too, is a natural bodily function required for survival. However, the arts of cooking so that food becomes tantalizing and of cultivating one's culinary skills and palate such that eating becomes a sensory delight change the experience entirely. There is quite a difference between eating scraps out of starvation or conversely, because one has a history of being force-fed such that food becomes repellant versus having the luxury of sitting down to a leisurely meal, prepared with loving attention to detail and in which the dishes reflect *your* particular food preferences. It is the difference between another predictable, reliable but not especially nutritious Big Mac versus a luxurious buffet, all arranged by a gourmet to display your favorite dishes. Each has been carefully selected, has a balance of visual and textural delights, the aromas designed to whet your appetites and the flavours caress or burst forth in your mouth. You want to linger over each bite or devour the whole meal, depending on your mood. There is nothing "natural" about cultivating gourmet cooking or tastes.

The client continues, "And in relationship after relationship, I've *never* wanted sex. Every relationship I've ever been in has ended because of my *problem.*" Sex therapists hear this phrase rather often. The presumption is that the speaker has a chronic problem of lack of sexual desire. The question, again, becomes: "But what is the nature of this sex you've never wanted?" Indeed, does the client have a disorder or a lifelong reluctance to settle for dismal sex? It is precisely because the higher desire partner(s) have attributed the end of the relationship to low sexual frequency that the individual fails to reckon – or more correctly, has no way of knowing – that just about all doomed relationships are relatively sexless in their final six months. Whatever the reasons that relationships ultimately end, it is cheap and easy to lay blame on lack of sex when the reality is that most people don't feel like having sex with each other when the relationship has gone downhill.

"I'm Just a Hopeless Case . . ."

The client continues, "And not only that . . . but in each relationship, *everything was fine at the beginning of the relationship* but the relationship ended as we kept arguing about frequency of sex . . ." How are we to understand this remark? In every respect, the beginnings of relationships are filled with promise. The old cliché about a new baby as a "bundle of joy" sounds utterly hackneyed until one holds one's own newborn in one's arms for the first time. The baby has yet to be shaped by the parents' (and others') mistakes; no damage has been done, yet. This child is pure, unspoiled potential. We can see whatever we would like to see in this little creation and no one can say otherwise. So it is with new relationships. We can project all our hopes and dreams onto one another . . . at least until we come to know one another. But until that happens, this relationship, too, is full of nothing but potential. In the world of polyamory, there is even a term for the exuberance that is characteristic of this phase: New Relationship Energy (NRE). In consensually non-monogamous relationships, it is wise not to bother getting jealous during this honeymoon phase because everyone knows it will fade once the lovers become better acquainted. That is, NRE diminishes once the exalted nature of one's aspirations are tainted by reality or to put it another way, once projections are withdrawn.

But there is another aspect of this comment, *"everything was fine at the beginning of the relationship"*, which couples report to their therapists commonly, even when the problem is unrelated to sexual frequency. At the beginning of relationships, couples take time to explore one another's bodies. They caress with curiosity and therefore, endlessly. They are interested enough to touch with leisure. And what a turn-on it is that someone whom you find attractive simultaneously finds you fascinating enough to want to get to know you. This is not limited to sex. At the outset, we are all questions: Where were you born? Tell me about your parents. What was your best subject in elementary school? What kind of music do you like? What's your favorite movie? And the answers are opportunities to tell the stories of who you are to this person for the first time, to present ourselves the way we most wish to be seen with no one to say, "Yes, you already told me at that story." So it is with sexual exploration: Early in the relationship, everything seems fresh and alive. There is nothing but opportunity for discovery. But in sex-negative cultures, most people stop exploring once they have ascertained the most expedient pathways to bring one another to orgasm efficiently (Kleinplatz, 1996a). Sex becomes goal-directed rather than pleasure-oriented. And then the real source of our disappointments quietly sets in; it was never that you found me so captivating. It wasn't that you found me endlessly fascinating. The end came as soon as you knew the quickest route to orgasm cold. As a woman articulated it in Chapter 10, her partner played her body like a pinball machine, leaving her feeling empty. The surest way to kill desire is to do what works – relentlessly (Kleinplatz, 1992).

The Pinball Wizard versus the Erotic Encounter

As our participants have indicated, expedient orgasms are not the route to optimal sexual experience. In fact, neither expediency nor orgasms may have much relevance for magnificent sex. It is precisely that one remains engaged and alert enough to what is most arousing to the partner in the moment that creates the sense of connection, desire and feeling desirable. The disadvantage to choosing the most expedient route to tension release, orgasm and intercourse, is that efforts aimed at efficiency may leave the individual with the sense of being in the hands of an expert at producing a predictable orgasm while being left with the feeling of being untouched (Kleinplatz, 1996b). The alternative to paint-by-numbers sex means not even looking for the formula to bring one's partner to orgasm as efficiently and predictably as possible. That same participant whose partner played her "like a pinball machine" later ended that relationship in favour of a partner with whom she could savour erotic delight.

So to come full circle, clients who proclaim that everything was fine in the beginning of each relationship but that towards the end, there were frequent arguments about decreasing frequency may be shining a spotlight on only the most obvious symptom of relationships in decay. McCarthy and McCarthy

(2020) suggest that the most common cause of low desire is disappointment. However, the disappointment may be in the dawning awareness of general disinterest in continuing to get to know one another. Once the partners have figured out how to run the household without acrimony and how to conduct a serviceable sex life, they literally settle down. Here is where we return to the lessons from our extraordinary lovers. Magnificent sex results from refusing to settle. That does not mean refusing to settle for a particular partner; it means refusing to settle for the minimal knowledge of one another required for normal sexual functioning and instead, to continue to search for the buried treasures that lie in each of us. These are gems, aspects of the self that are merely glimpsed as they glisten in the half-light of burgeoning relationships but can truly shine as they are polished in the erotic intimacy of growing relationships.

But No Really . . . In the Beginning of Our Relationship It All Seemed So Easy, So Natural and Spontaneous

"And whenever we were together we just seemed to fall into each other's arms effortlessly . . ." Early on in new relationships, partners always seem to be in synch and sex seems to come "naturally and spontaneously". This, of course, is at least partially an illusion. The reality is a bit more complex. In Chapter 3, we debunked this myth with the words of the many extraordinary lovers who emphasized the role of intentionality in creating magnificent sex in long-term relationships. But the reason couples seemed to be in synch at the outset is because each individual has focused a great deal of emotional attention and energy on the other and so what affects one, the other, or the budding relationship predominates in setting their moods. It is the mutual attention that has them seemingly in synch. This is an important lesson for future stages of the relationship. Most of the people, most of the time are forced eventually to focus their attentions on jobs, children, finances and running their households. The insights from extraordinary lovers suggest that relationships require ongoing maintenance, care and attention carved out deliberately or they will be unable to thrive.

As for the notion that romance and sex should be "natural and spontaneous", think back to all the effort that was required to create the illusion in question. In a new relationship, people live apart. That means they can spend their days carefully planning to look effortless. Yes, they did work all day. Nonetheless, they sent messages to one another to prime the pump. After work, they came home; took off their clothes, especially the grungy, graying underwear with the loose elastics, hid the dirty dishes and the laundry (extraordinary lovers often mentioned that putting away the laundry made for a more inviting bedroom and thus became an element of their preparations); showered, shaved and groomed; brushed their teeth; put on fresh new underthings and clothes that made them feel presentable and confident, if not outright sexy and desirable; blow-dried and styled their hair; applied whatever "product", scent and cosmetics added to their feelings of allure . . . and so, when the appointed time came, after day-long preparations, they were able to *appear* "natural and spontaneous". One cannot pull off that sort of illusion when sharing a domicile. The effort will be visible.

But who is to say that showing one's efforts is a bad thing? The people we interviewed spoke of the importance of preparation, whether physical preparation, preparation of the environment or interpersonal preparation so as to enable them to be in a welcoming mood for one another. If we want sex to happen at all in long-term relationships, it will take effort. If we want sex to be optimal, it will take considerable time, effort and energy which is to be understood as evidence of one's ongoing commitment to making sex fulfilling, rather than taking it – or one's partner(s) and their interest or availability – for granted.

If couples want to recapture or go beyond the calibre of sex they recall from courtship days, they will need to expend at least as much energy as they did once to making their wishes a reality. It should not feel like work but it surely will require devotion.

Creating Space – Not "Date Night"

This entails learning from extraordinary lovers who put considerable attention towards creating physical and psychological spaces which bring about the possibility of magnificent sex. This is conceptually different from "date night". If anything, the notion of "date night" in isolation is counterproductive. I [P.J.K.] see more disappointed couples in my office on February 15, the morning after Valentine's Day, than any other day of the year. It is the imperative to have romantic sex regardless of the circumstances that is so oppressive as to backfire. Each individual needs to determine what the prerequisites might be for optimal sexual experience. Please note, the operative word here is "optimal" rather than "sexual". The question is not what items you need to clear off your to-do list in order to gear up for the possibility of having sex.

Instead, the question is what do you need to do within, with/in your body and in your physical and interpersonal environment in order to create the psychological and physical space that would be conducive to enabling sex to be magnificent? This requires being deliberate, each investing in mutual good-will and following through on one's intentions. Of equal importance, what do the partners need to say and do to clear up any unresolved conflicts? It is important to recognize the connections between negative interactions and how a negative comment can lead to hurt feelings, and from there to further negative comments and ultimately to withdrawal (literally or figuratively). The existence of a positive, upward cycle where good feelings can build on each other, where erotic intimacy can build the relationship and the relationship can build the quality of sex, represents the flip side of the death spiral.

The lesson here is that attention to creating helpful preparatory conditions is a necessary prerequisite for optimal erotic intimacy. Does this guarantee that magnificent sex will occur? No, there is no guarantee. However, it does create the right circumstances for enabling magic to sometimes ensue.

Extraordinary Sexual Communication: By Word and by Deed

Couples and sex therapists are generally well-trained at teaching couples the skills of effective communication. Across the board and different theoretical orientations (e.g., Gottman, 1999; Gottman & Silver, 2015; Schnarch, 2009), therapists recognize that there is a limit to how far merely "effective" communication strategies will take a couple in a crunch, whether that critical situation is a heated fight or an erotic moment of truth.

Please review *any* of the quotations from our participants. With few exceptions, their words are extraordinary. Their level of authentic and transparent communication far exceeds merely effective communication. They are master communicators. Regardless of educational or socioeconomic background, age or sex, they were remarkably honest, clear, forthcoming and spoke vividly, if not poetically. For us [P.J.K. and A.D.M.], having had the opportunity to interview these individuals was quite simply a blessing. Imagine what it is like to be in bed with a partner who is willing to tell you – and when that won't work, to literally show you – what exactly it is that is desired in the moment. That takes courage. Even, "A little to the right . . . now harder . . . now slower . . . Let's switch positions . . . Now whatever you do, just *please, don't stop!*" is daunting for most of the people most of the time.

This requires some serious introspection and decision-making about how much you care to share, whether in speaking or listening and whether in touching or being touched.

Now it gets really scary: No one can tell you how to do it. That is both the good news and the unnerving news. Only you can decide how much of yourself you wish to reveal with your words and your silence. Only you can decide whether you choose to listen between the lines to your partner's intent with goodwill when your partner is verbally clumsy and fumbling in bed or to feign perplexity. Entrusting another with one's hidden fears and hopes is an act of courage. Too many are afraid that the acceptance they crave will not be forthcoming if they disclose their secrets. The power we grant to our lovers when we share our deepest sexual fantasies is so great that few dare to do so (Kleinplatz, 1992).

Then it gets harder yet: No matter how many books you read and videos you watch, there is no correct way to caress another person. There are correct techniques for how to change your spark plugs or perform an appendectomy. The "right way" in bed is the way that is called for in the lover's body in *this* moment. And just because it is perfect tonight does not mean it will be perfect tomorrow. It is useful to have some basic, working knowledge of your partner's body or your partners' particular preferences. However, bodies have moods. Do not take this personally – it is not a reflection on your skill as a lover. The perfect dessert of tiramisu gelato on a hot summer's night may not be what you crave after dinner in January. This means remaining attuned and sensitive continually to expressing and receiving your partner's wishes in the moment, communicated verbally and via touch.

I [P.J.K.] have heard too many clients complain about being touched by rote in bed repeatedly. "I swear, whether she's rubbing my tired shoulders or my ass or my penis, she does it like she's just polishing wood: It's just back and forth and back and forth, stroking my back the same way she does my balls. [He motions as if to demonstrate polishing a piece of furniture.] She doesn't seem to pay attention to *me* at all."

Correspondingly, how willing are we to allow ourselves to be felt while being touched? Physicians are taught to look for signs of what is referred to as "guarding" when they examine a patient's abdomen for non-specific complaints of belly pain. The way one's belly responds as the physician palpates or pokes around the area provides some of the clinical data needed for diagnosis, some of which comes from observation of "guarding", that is, involuntary tightening of the body when warding off pain. One can reframe what used to be called vaginismus, now referred to as the muscular tensing and tightening part of genital pelvic pain penetration disorder (GPPPD) as the woman's body guarding at the prospect of penetration. Try to recall the way your own body felt and reacted from within the last time a physician approached you to perform some unpleasant examination. Imagine how your body might freeze while being sexually assaulted. Now try to recall what it was like touching your partner or being touched when one or both of you was not keen on or down-right reluctant to proceed in having sex. What would it take for you to make your body open and penetrable (whether literally or figuratively) so that your partner could really feel what's taking place within you while touching you? Again, there is no general, correct answer, but if you are honest enough with yourself, you will know what you need personally, interpersonally and in terms of the nature of the sexual contact, before you will allow yourself to be felt through and through while being touched. What would make it worth your while? Only you know the answer. Count on the answer changing over time.

What Can We Learn from Our Fondest Memories to Fuel Our Most Cherished Hopes?

The extraordinary lovers in our research were not only remarkable communi-cators; they were also wonderfully authentic, transparent and self-aware. How might others emulate these qualities? How can even those who are dubious about ever recapturing desire discover what possibilities may still lie within? If you are willing, you may wish to try the following exercise. (If you are a thera-pist, consider suggesting this exercise for individuals or couples, with or without desire problems, who want to enhance their sex lives; see Kleinplatz, 2016.) Set 20 minutes or so aside to be alone with your imagination, plus a paper and pen-cil. Try to recall your three favorite sexual memories. They need not conform to conventional definitions of "sexual" events nor involve genital contact; you will recognize when you have located them because they involve feeling fully alive in your skin. (The memories might not involve a current partner.) You need not share the content of these memories with anyone (including your partners or therapist, if applicable). Write down a few words for each memory so that you can identify them later. Then try to find your three favorite sexual fantasies. Again, how you define both "sexual" and "fantasies" is entirely up to you. You know these fantasies. These are your "go to" images that you always count on when you're in the middle of solo or partnered sex and just can't seem to get over the edge. You are so close but will need to conjure up your old, reliable fantasies that will do it for you every time. Now that you've identified them, jot down a few key words to keep track of each fantasy. For some individuals, their most cherished memories have also become their favorite fantasies. Given the overlap, they will therefore, have a total of three, rather than six items listed. In any case, examine the list carefully to see what elements they have in common. Study them without judgment. What do they reveal? Allow yourself to be surprised. Now what have you just discovered about what is erotic for you? What is distinctive about the sex of your dreams? What would it take to make these dreams a reality? What obstacles stand in the way of living these dreams and how could these be overcome?

The "Cure" for "Low Desire/Frequency" Is Creating Desirable Sex

Clients who report low libido and their spouses often present with a tally of how frequently they had sex, who initiated what and then disagree about frequency. However, it may be more helpful to treat frequency as a red herring. Instead of being trapped into treating the "disorder" – or even the symptom of the alleged disorder – it may be more helpful for the clinician to change the conversation from quantity to the quality of sexual experiences. Shifting the focus from frequency to quality could help individuals and couples focus on the kind of sex they want and whether it fills their needs. The data we have amassed from extraordinary lovers on how to bring about optimal erotic intimacy may help to answer patients' unasked but desperate questions.

Over 25 years ago, in the course of conducting an assessment with a couple newly referred for treatment of low sexual frequency, I [P.J.K.] commented casually, "Well I rather like sex but if I had the kind of sex you've been having, I wouldn't want it either." Their response was utter relief. Clients who have sexual problems often enter therapists' offices feeling defective and in need of repair. The irony is that their lack of desire is an indicator of psychosexual health; they have low desire for lousy sex. Therapists often attempt to downplay disappointment and to lower sexual expectations, for example, by normalizing the decreasing frequency of their sexual activities in a long-term relationship. Instead, therapists might want to consider that there is something powerful and affirming about acknowledging that sometimes, lack of interest in sex is evidence of good judgment (Kleinplatz, 1992, 2006, 2016). Most of us grow up hearing that we must wait to have sex until we marry, or at the very least, until we are older or meet the right person. After years of waiting eagerly, too many find themselves perplexed and disenchanted, asking in effect, "Is that all there is?" This can be a useful starting place. The alternative to disillusionment is daring to dream of sex worth wanting so that one never feels tempted to settle again.

Welcome to Hogwarts

If you recall the Harry Potter series, the first time our hero enters Hogwarts, he must make his way to the Gryffindor common room. However, as he and his friends quickly discover, the staircase headed upwards is moving even as he is attempting to climb. Furthermore, he will need to jump rather quickly from one moving staircase to another with no assurance that it will be the correct or the final leap in order to eventually reach the entrance to his destination. So it is for therapists and clients in dealing with problems as complex as low/no desire and low/no frequency. Our data suggest that manualized treatments for the complex problems of low/no desire and low/no frequency will not work. One-size-fits-all methods cannot be expected to be effective with concerns as multifaceted as desire. Therapists and clients will need to be prepared to embark on a journey where the pathway is unknown; the ground is literally shifting beneath their feet as they attempt to move forward; and find the courage – if they are willing – to continue climbing upwards even as their view of the peak changes as they draw near.

This is how we were feeling as we began to devise a clinical approach to find out whether the lessons from extraordinary lovers were merely aspirational models or whether any old person (literally, or perhaps even some younger folks) might also be able to enhance their sex lives in substantive and fundamental ways.

Can We Inspire/Teach Better Sex?

The team's objective by 2012 was to develop a clinical approach based on the findings described thus far. The discoveries that came from studying extraordinary lovers had impressed us but would we be able to use them to craft a psychotherapy intervention that could change the sex lives of people struggling with no or low desire/frequency?

Although most treatment for couples with sexual desire discrepancy is focused on treating the lower-desire individual, our approach would eschew that mindset and instead highlight the discoveries and lessons we had encountered that governed individuals while in erotically intimate relationships. Our team knew that the basis for any intervention would need to encompass the following principles, considerations and goals:

- To expand capacities for intense and overwhelming pleasure
- To cultivate erotic willingness

- To seek out the sexual experiences they crave
- To enable clients to become more comfortable in their own skin, fully embodied and absorbed in the moment
- To embrace their vulnerability while being present in the moment
- To have intimate knowledge of themselves and what makes them feel alive sexually and how to express this *with* another
- To develop comfort with self and other to the point that imperfections and vulnerability are not threatening *with* another
- To allow for full authenticity, aliveness, openness to experience, embodiment and connection and trust *with* another
- To discard masks (uncover), to lay themselves bare, to risk being seen and known as they truly are *with* another
- To create intrapsychic and interpersonal safety to access and reveal deepest vulnerabilities together
- To connect with their partner(s) fully and deeply
- To attain crucial skills: Mutual empathy and simultaneously being connected in the moment *with* another
- To discover ways of communicating via touch that would allow individuals and partners to touch so as to feel and to be touched so as to be felt and metaphorically penetrated
- To use conflict so as to increase intimacy together
- To each be able to take risks in an atmosphere of *just enough* safety (if you're doing it right, it should feel at least a little scary)
- To take a broader focus than is typical with sex therapy interventions (that is, individual, relational, before/during/after sex)

Our understanding was that similar – though not usually identical – skills and principles are common objectives in individual sex therapy, for example, teaching people who are sexually dysfunctional and easily distracted to be mindful. Since the dawn of sex therapy, exercises to re-claim touch without engendering performance anxiety (i.e., sensate focus) have been a classic technique (Masters & Johnson, 1970). Improving interpersonal communication skills and teaching clients how to fight fair are a standard intervention in couples therapy. Our objectives were, obviously, farther reaching and we aspired higher.

We also had an additional consideration which is not particularly related to anything else in our research: We believe strongly in social justice and that couples-sex therapy should be accessible to all. Neither sex nor couples therapy is covered by health insurance plans in many locations, especially in the United States. Masters and Johnson's (1970) treatment model required that patients come to St. Louis and stay in a hotel near their clinic for two weeks. Very few therapists, if any, continue to require that couples in treatment live in relative isolation from the pressures of children, work and household maintenance – which require unusual financial and other resources, not to mention very high motivation. (Some continue to offer short-term therapy "retreats", often held at luxury resorts.) Nonetheless, the cost for individuals or couples in meeting alone with a couples-sex therapist can be prohibitive. It was important to us that any approach be time-effective and affordable. There was also a long history in sex therapy of using group modalities effectively for sex therapy, albeit usually for treating the identified patient alone. Group therapy has been employed in dealing with sexual concerns since the inception of sex therapy (e.g., Barbach, 1980, 2000; Brotto et al., 2015; Ogden, 2012; Zilbergeld, 1980, 1999) and has been shown to be effective at normalizing sexual concerns, thus alleviating the burden of change (Dodson, 2012; Wolberg & Aronson, 1975). As such, our team aimed to develop a *group* therapy approach for couples founded on the lessons from extraordinary lovers.

Group-Couples Therapy for Couples with No to Low Sexual Desire/Frequency and Sexual Desire Discrepancy

If our participants were correct in relaying that great lovers are made, not born, then perhaps we could impart what we had learned from them. In 2012, we developed a group therapy approach for couples dealing with no/low sexual desire/frequency and sexual desire discrepancy. The group therapy model followed the major principles in the approach of Irvin Yalom (Yalom & Leszcz, 2005). That meant that our ideal group size was to consist of eight to twelve individuals or four to six couples. The eight sessions were to correspond generally to the eight components and seven categories of facilitating factors of optimal sexual experience as identified in our previous qualitative work (Kleinplatz, Ménard, Paquet et al., 2009; Ménard et al., 2015). That meant developing an eight-week, 16-hour, couples-group-therapy approach which would allow couples time to process between weekly sessions.

We developed a paradigm that highlighted looking within, becoming centered, authenticity and focusing on optimal personal development (e.g., Gendlin, 1978a, 1978b, 1996; Mahrer, 2008, 2009; Perls, 1969), alongside active and receptive communication, heightened empathy with words and sensitivity via touch (e.g., Aron et al. 1997; Chaitow, 2003; Gottman & Silver, 2015; Mahrer, 2004; Mahrer, Boulet & Fairweather, 1994; McCarthy & McCarthy, 2020). Our primary modality was Experiential (Mahrer, 2004; Mahrer & Boulet, 2001). Our mottos were borrowed from Fritz Perls, founder of Gestalt psychotherapy, who wrote (1971), "Lose your mind and come to your senses" as well as our own, *"Just safe enough . . ."* recognizing the complementary roles of personal autonomy and interpersonal trust in erotic risk-taking. We emphasized the dual skills of intense embodiment within *while* being fully, empathically connected with the partner in the moment. The exercises during the sessions included, for example, challenging sexual myths and Focusing (Gendlin, 1978a, 1996; not to be confused with Masters and Johnson's sensate focus exercises). The fifth session, to be conducted by a professor of massage therapy, research team member Danielle Pratt, RMT, focused on the experience of heightened sensitivity while touching and being touched. The emphasis was on paying attention to what felt pleasurable right then and there – with the recognition that it would fluctuate from moment to moment – rather than some a priori set of skills for touching "correctly". No sexual activity was to take place at any point in the group nor any assigned between sessions. We did assign homework such as readings, exercises for enhancing playfulness, encouraging vulnerability, deepening trust or watching videos we had developed for this therapy.

We were ready to conduct our first group and had only to determine the inclusion and exclusion criteria. Clinical trials were ongoing at that time for Flibanserin (trade name, Addyi) and we examined the extensive exclusion criteria (e.g., sexual dysfunction, a prior history of low desire; relationship problems, partner's psychological or sexual dysfunction; major life stress) for development of that drug, intended for treatment of low desire in women (FDA, 2015). Given that we wanted to remain as accessible as possible, we decided to exclude only individuals who were using prescription drugs known to cause sexual desire problems, for example, certain classes of antidepressants (i.e., selective serotonin reuptake inhibitors) and specific, hormonal contraceptives such as Depo-Provera. After a year of assessing men and women for our groups, every couple had been rejected based on this criterion alone. We then eliminated this criterion, included prospective patients regardless of medications and had several groups filled quickly.

In summary, inclusion criteria were being heterosexual or LGBTQ in a relationship where one or the other or both are distressed by low desire or low frequency of sex, usually both. Exclusion criteria were existing domestic abuse (i.e., current physical violence in the home) or being at the point of filing for divorce.

Long-time research team member, psychotherapist Nicolas Paradis, M.Ed., and I [P.J.K.] were ready to begin working as co-therapists, to be followed by other co-therapist dyads from within the team. With the encouragement of Aleksandar Štulhofer, Ph.D., the researcher who had developed the New Sexual Satisfaction Scale (NSSS; Štulhofer, Busko & Brouillard, 2010, 2011), we began using the NSSS as a pre-test, post-test and six-month follow-up measure of change before and after participation, as well as patient/client written feedback about changes in their sex lives since beginning couples group therapy. The NSSS has been identified as a psychometrically sound measure of sexual satisfaction with strong internal reliability, high test-retest reliability and good convergent validity (Mark et al., 2014). Unlike most measures, its items are directly related to the higher end of the spectrum of sexual experience (rather than average function versus dysfunction). The NSSS was chosen because its items measure the elements (e.g., emotional opening up during sex) identified as crucial among extraordinary lovers. The NSSS also included items measuring satisfaction with frequency and initiation, which are precisely the concerns reported by couples distressed by desire and frequency problems. By the time our team had conducted several groups in 2015, we had the answer to the empirical question: Yes, what we had learned from extraordinary lovers was transferable to others, specifically couples with low/no sexual desire/frequency, and had made a clinically significant and measurable impact on the quality of their sex lives. By 2018, our team had begun the translation phase of the research. That is, our team in Ottawa began training therapists in other parts of Canada and the United States to ensure that others, too, would obtain the same outcomes and effect sizes in conducting therapy in their own cities. Their post-test and six-month follow-up data paralleled our own on the NSSS (Kleinplatz et al., 2018, in press). Interestingly, the items on which we consistently see the greatest improvement across therapists and across groups are "intensity of sexual arousal", "focus/concentration during sexual activity", "emotional opening up during sex", "the pleasure I provide to my partner", the "balance between what I give and receive during sex", "initiation of sexual activity", "sexual creativity", "variety of sexual activities" and "frequency of sexual activity". Most of all, group therapy clients also reported being more satisfied with their sex lives overall recently. That is, the item measuring overall satisfaction with one's sex life showed the largest increase and the largest effect size.

Did the couples in our latest clinical studies have magnificent sex? Perhaps, but if the extraordinary lovers we began interviewing a decade earlier were correct, optimal sexual experiences require considerable time, attention and even devotion. We did not expect them to have optimal erotic intimacy after only 16 hours, but the clients in couples group therapy did substantially begin the journey towards creating more fulfilling and desirable sex lives. They had changed their relationships, making them just safe enough to risk emotionally. They also acquired the intentionality, playfulness, empathic communication and other skills and knowledge of the further efforts to be expended as they mature if their sex lives are to continue to grow more and more rewarding.

We are continuing this work in couples-group therapy internationally and welcome the opportunity to collaborate. Please see our website at optimalsexualexperiences.com and feel free to contact us. We are excited about what we have learned from extraordinary lovers, remain grateful for what they have shared with us, are delighted that it can enhance others' sex lives and are eager to share it further.

14
CONCLUSIONS

So where does all of this information about magnificent sexual encounters leave us? What is the before and after of this book? We have traversed a lot of territory here and hope we have convinced readers to rethink their beliefs about the nature of and contributors to "great sex", and possibly even about the nature of sex itself. As we discovered through our interviews, optimal sexual experiences bear almost no relation to media and pop culture depictions. They are also barely connected to academic conceptualizations, which tend to go from "dysfunctional" to "functional" and then to stop short.

The results of our research suggest that sex is both less (i.e., less constricting, less formulaic, less genitally-oriented) and more (i.e., more open to everyone, more freeing) than these myths would have us believe.

Magnificent sex is not the stuff of tips, tricks and techniques shown in movies of young lovers. No, it is much better than that: It's the stuff that dreams are made of and when cultivated, it can grow over a lifetime. It does not happen "naturally and spontaneously" but it is possible with concerted time, energy and effort. More than even that, extraordinary lovers had to want it, intend to make it a reality, practise and nurture the qualities that help to create optimal erotic intimacy. There are those who focus much of their attention on how to meet fully in the flesh in the moment. Those who envisioned it made memorable sex a reality, by creating the right circumstances, making themselves physically and emotionally available, seeking out the right partner(s), choosing to make their wishes known and so on.

Optimal sexual experiences involve being totally absorbed and immersed in the moment, an intense connection, being erotically intimate with another person, communicating empathically, taking risks, surrendering to one another, being authentic and accepting the very real possibility of transcendence and transformation. How does one get there? Luckily, there are many routes up the mountain and no one route is correct (or faster). It may involve focusing on letting go of early messages and unlearning and maturing. It may involve developing centering skills and increasing comfort with oneself. It may involve applying all of that awareness during a sexual encounter, which may feel like an altogether greater and riskier challenge. Other routes up the mountain may require partners, although their identities could include friends, play partners or a long-term spouse. Developing an atmosphere of trust may allow for greater authenticity, and from there to greater honesty about true desires, and from there, to greater risk-taking and exploration in the moment. Together, getting to the peak might require developing deeper empathy, deliberately building an atmosphere of trust or playfully exploring and venturing into new but enticing territory. It may involve consciously cultivating pleasure, intensity, passion and eroticism during sex, while also leaning into the possibilities of connecting, going with the flow and getting swept up together. It may involve different combinations of these approaches at different points across the lifespan. Above all, navigating the paths up the mountain so as to find the best route will likely require some devotion to climbing the mountain and seeing the view for oneself.

It is time for sexologists to change our models to better reflect the experiences of individuals across the life cycle. Sexologists need to re-evaluate their understanding of the spectrum of sexuality; to do otherwise means ignoring a wealth of information that could potentially be of great help to clients and the general public. This means that, like extraordinary lovers, we too will need to re-vision sexuality. And correspondingly, clinicians will need to acquire new skill sets and learn how to develop new capacities in our clients (e.g., thought-stopping versus being utterly embodied while intimately engaged).

The good news remains (Kleinplatz & Ménard, 2007) that being sexually functional is not necessary for optimal sexual experiences; the "bad" news is that being sexually functional is not sufficient for optimal sexual experiences. Magnificent sex requires growing beyond the conventional sex scripts most people learn in their youth. Disappointing sex lives can change. The goal here is not merely to discard sex guilt, shame and inhibition. Rather, it is to jettison the entire aspirational package of paint-by-numbers sex (Kleinplatz, 1996b).

We now know that this works. Erotic intimacy is within reach. Our most recent studies demonstrate these findings can benefit old, young, LGBTQ, straight, able-bodied, disabled, monogamous, consensually non-monogamous, kinky and vanilla people to enhance the quality of their erotic intimacy impressively and significantly. The rest of the news is that these kinds of experiences take deliberate and intentional time and effort. Optimal sexual experiences require a choice to proceed up the mountain and a willingness to take on the challenges that arise. This can be risky and will certainly involve some discomfort (although likely growth, too). However, the alternative is risky as well, as we have seen among those pulled down into the sexual relationship death spiral.

Although each individual and couple might need to find their own pathways up the mountain, some extraordinary lovers have pointed out a few trails. So we leave that choice with you. But for those who are willing to climb, we promise that the views are magnificent.

Resources

To Locate a Certified Sex Therapist:

The Board of Examiners in Sex Therapy and Counselling of Ontario
www.BESTCO.info

American Association of Sex Educators Counselors and Therapists
www.AASECT.org

Therapy, Training and Research on Optimal Sexual Experiences:

www.optimalsexualexperiences.com

Major Sexology Associations and Opportunities for Continuing Education:

Sex Information and Education Council of Canada
www.sieccan.org/

Annual Guelph Conference and Training Institute on Sexuality
www.guelphsexualityconference.ca/

The Society for the Scientific Study of Sexuality (SSSS)
www.sexscience.org/

Society for Sex Therapy and Research
www.sstarnet.org

American Association of Sex Educators Counselors and Therapists
www.AASECT.org

International Society for the Study of Women's Sexual Health
www.isswsh.org

International Society for Sexual Medicine
www.issm.org/

Diverse Sexualities Research and Education Institute
www.dsrei.org

Guidelines to Distinguish between Consensual BDSM versus Abuse:

https://secureservercdn.net/198.71.233.68/9xj.1d5.myftpupload.com/wp-content/uploads/2019/12/NCSF_Consent_Negotiation.pdf

https://secureservercdn.net/198.71.233.68/9xj.1d5.myftpupload.com/wp-content/uploads/2019/12/BDSM-vs-Abuse-Statement.pdf

Sexual Aids (toys) for People Who are Disabled and Chronically Ill:

www.comeasyouare.com

Bibliography for Relationships and Therapy

Barbach, L. (2000). *For yourself: The fulfillment of female sexuality*. New York, NY: Signet Books.

Barker, M. (2012). *Rewriting the rules: An integrative guide to love, sex and relationships*. New York, NY: Routledge.

Bouman, W. & Kleinplatz, P. J. (2015). (Eds.) *Sexuality and ageing*. New York, NY: Routledge.

Braun-Harvey, D. & Vigorito, M. A. (2016). *Treating out of control sexual behavior: Rethinking sex addiction*. New York, NY: Springer.

Butler, R. N. & Lewis, M. I. (2002). *The new love and sex after 60*. New York, NY: Ballantine Books.

Dodson, B. (2012). Orgasms for two. http://dodsonandross.com/tag/orgasms-two

Ellison, C. R. (2000). *Women's sexualities*. Oakland, CA: New Harbinger.

Foley, S. (2005). *Sex and love for grownups: A no-nonsense guide to a life of passion*. New York, NY: AARP.

Foley, S., Kope, S. A. & Sugrue, D. (2012). *Sex matters for women*. New York, NY: Guilford.

Golden, G. H. (2009). *In the grip of desire: A therapist at work with sexual secrets*. New York, NY: Routledge.

Goldstein, A. T., Pukall, C. F. & Goldstein, I. (2011). *When sex hurts: A woman's guide to banishing sexual pain*. Cambridge, MA: DaCapoPress.

Gottman, J. & Silver, N. (2015). *The seven principles for making marriage work*. New York, NY: Harmony Books.

Joannides, P. (2016). *The guide to getting it on*. 7th edition. Waldport, OR: Goofy Foot Press.

Johnson, S. M. (2008). *Hold me tight*. New York, NY: Little, Brown & Co.

Katz, A. (2009). *Women, cancer, sex*. Pittsburgh, PA: Hygeia Media.

Katz, A. (2009). *Men, cancer, sex*. Pittsburgh, PA: Hygeia Media.

Kaufman, M., Silverberg, C. & Odette, F. (2007). *The ultimate guide to sex and disability*. San Francisco, CA: Cleis Press.

Kerner, I. (2004). *She comes first: The thinking man's guide to pleasuring a woman*. New York, NY: HarperCollins.

Kleinplatz, P. J. (Ed.) (2012). *New directions in sex therapy: Innovations and alternatives.* New York, NY: Routledge.

Kliger, L. & Nedelman, D. (2006). *Still sexy after all these years? The 9 unspoken truths about women's desire beyond 50.* New York, NY: Penguin.

Komarisuk, B. R., Beyer-Flores, C. & Whipple, B. (2006). *The science of orgasm.* Baltimore, MD: Johns Hopkins Press, 2006.

Leight, A. K. (2013). *Sex happens: The gay man's guide to creative intimacy.* Minneapolis, MN: Langdon Press.

Ley, D. M. (2012). *The myth of sex addiction.* Lanham, MD: Rowman & Littlefield.

Mahrer, A. R. (2007). *The other deeper you.* Ottawa, Canada: University of Ottawa Press.

Mahrer, A. R. (2008). *The manual of optimal behaviour.* Laval, QC: HG Publications.

Mahrer, A. R. (2009). *The optimal person.* Laval, QC: HG Publications.

Maltz, W. (2012). *The sexual healing journey: A guide for survivors of sexual abuse.* New York, NY: HarperCollins.

Manley, G. T. (2013). *Assisted loving: The journey through sexuality and aging.* Cambridge, MA: Westview Press.

McCarthy, B. & McCarthy, E. (2009). *Discovering your couple sexual style.* New York, NY: Brunner-Routledge.

McCarthy, B. & McCarthy, E. (2020). *Rekindling desire: A step-by-step program to help low-sex and no-sex marriages.* 3rd edition. New York, NY: Routledge.

McCarthy, B. & Metz, M. E. (2008). *Men's sexual health: Fitness for satisfying sex.* New York, NY: Routledge.

Metz, M. E. & McCarthy, B. (2010). *Enduring desire: Your guide to lifelong intimacy.* New York: Routledge.

Mintz, L. (2017). *Becoming cliterate: Why orgasm equality matters – and how to get it.* New York, NY: HarperCollins.

Moser, C. (1999). *Health care without shame: A handbook for the sexually diverse and their caregivers.* San Francisco, CA: Greenery Press.

Moser, C. (2020). *Sex positive healthcare.* San Francisco, CA: Greenery Press.

Nagoski, E. (2015). *Come as you are.* New York, NY: Simon & Schuster.

Ogden, G. (1999). *Women who love sex.* Boston, MA: Womanspirit Press.

Perel, E. (2006). *Mating in captivity: Reconciling the erotic and the domestic.* New York, NY: Harper Collins.

Price, J. (2011). *Naked at our age: Talking out loud about senior sex.* New York, NY: Seal Press.

Resnick, S. (2012). *The heart of desire: Keys to the pleasures of love.* New York, NY: Wiley.

Schnarch, D. (1997). *Passionate marriage: Love, sex, and intimacy in emotionally committed relationships.* New York, NY: Wiley.

Taoromino, T. (2008). *Opening up: A guide to creating and sustaining open relationships.* New York, NY: Cleis.

Zilbergeld, B. (1999). *The new male sexuality.* New York, NY: Bantam Books.

Zilbergeld, B. (2004). *Better than ever: Love and sex at midlife.* Norwalk, CT: Crown House Publishing.

References

Alexander, M. G. & Fisher, T. D. (2003). Truth and consequences: Using the bogus pipeline to examine sex differences in self-reported sexuality. *Journal of Sex Research*, 40(1), 27–35. doi: 10.1080/00224490309552164

American Psychiatric Association (2013). *Diagnostic and statistical manual of mental disorders*. 5th edition. Washington, DC: APA.

Aron, A., Melinat, E., Aron, E. N., Vallone, R. D. & Bator, R. J. (1997). The experimental generation of interpersonal closeness: A procedure and some preliminary findings. *Personality and Social Psychology Bulletin*, 23(4), 363–377.

Barbach, L. (1980). *Women discover orgasm*. New York, NY: Free Press.

Barbach, L. (2000). *For yourself: The fulfillment of female sexuality*. New York, NY: Signet Books.

Barker, M. J., Gill, R. & Harvey, L. (2018). Mediated intimacy: Sex advice in media culture. *Sexualities*, 21(8), 1337–1345. doi: 10.1177/1363460718781342

Basson, R. (2001). Using a different model for female sexual response to address women's problematic low sexual desire. *Journal of Sex and Marital Therapy*, 27(5), 395–403.

Basson, R. (2002). A model of women's sexual arousal. *Journal of Sex and Marital Therapy*, 28(1), 1–10.

Basson, R. (2005). Women's sexual dysfunction: Revised and expanded definitions. *Canadian Medical Association Journal*, 172, 1327–1333.

Basson, R. (2010). Women's difficulties with low sexual desire, sexual avoidance, and sexual aversion. In S. B. Levine, C. B. Risen & S. E. Althof (Eds.), *Handbook of clinical sexuality for mental health professionals*. 2nd edition (pp. 159–179). New York, NY: Routledge/ Taylor & Francis.

Bowen, M. (1978). *Family therapy in clinical practice*. New York, NY: Jason Aronson.

Bowlby, J. M. (1969). *Attachment and loss*, Vol. 1: *Attachment*. New York, NY: Basic Books.

Broder, M. & Goldman, A. (2004). *Secrets of sexual ecstasy*. New York, NY: Penguin Group Inc.

Brotto, L. (2018). *Better sex through mindfulness*. Vancouver, BC: Greystone.

Brotto, L. A., Basson, R., Smith, K. B., Driscoll, M. & Sadownik, L. (2015). Mindfulness-based group therapy for women with provoked vestibulodynia. *Mindfulness*, 6(3), 417–432.

Cabrera, C. & Ménard, A. D. (2012). "She exploded into a million pieces": A qualitative and quantitative examination of orgasm descriptions in contemporary romance novels. *Sexuality & Culture*, 17, 193–212. doi: 10.1007/s12119-012-9147-0

Califia, P. (1994). *Public sex: The culture of radical sex*. San Francisco, CA: Cleis.

Castleman, M. (2004). *Great sex*. New York, NY: Rodale Inc.

Centers for Disease Control and Prevention (2017). *Sexually Transmitted Disease Surveillance 2016*. Atlanta: U.S. Department of Health and Human Services.

Centers for Disease Control and Prevention (2018). Reported STDs in the United States, 2018. https://www.cdc.gov/nchhstp/newsroom/docs/factsheets/std-trends-508.pdf

Chaitow, L. (2003). *Palpation and assessment skills: Assessment through touch*. 2nd edition. London: Churchill Livingstone, Elsevier.

Charest, M. & Kleinplatz, P. J. (2018). A review of recent innovations in the treatment of low sexual desire. *Current Sexual Health Reports*. doi: 10.1007/s11930-018-0171-4

Choudhri, Y., Miller, J., Sandhu, J., Leon, A. & Aho, J. (2018a). Gonorrhea in Canada, 2010–2015. *Canada Communicable Disease Report*, 44, 37–42.

Choudhri, Y., Miller, J., Sandhu, J., Leon, A. & Aho J. (2018b). Chlamydia in Canada, 2010–2015. *Canada Communicable Disease Report*, 44, 49–54.

Choudhri, Y., Miller, J., Sandhu, J., Leon, A. & Aho, J. (2018c). Infectious and congenital syphilis in Canada, 2010–2015. *Canada Communicable Disease Report*, 44, 43–48.

Csíkszentmihályi, M. (1990). *Flow. The psychology of optimal experience*. New York, NY: Harper & Row.

DeLamater, J. & Koepsel, E. (2015). Relationships and sexual expression in later life: A biopsychosocial perspective. *Sexual and Relationship Therapy*, 30(1), 37–59.

Dodson, B. (2012). Orgasms for two. Retrieved from http://dodsonandross.com/tag/orgasms-two

Duran, R. L. & Prusank, D. T. (1997). Relational themes in men's and women's popular nonfiction magazine articles. *Journal of Social and Personal Relationships*, 14, 165–189.

Emanuel, P. J. (2014). Sex and the single senior. *New York Times*. January 18. Retrieved from http://www.NYTimes.com/2014/01/19/opinion/Sunday/emanual-sex-and-the-single-senior.html?_r=zero

Farb, N. (2014). From retreat center to clinic to boardroom? Perils and promises of the modern mindfulness movement. *Religions*, 5, 1062–1086.

Ferenidou, F., Kapoteli, V., Moisidis, K., Koutsogiannis, I., Giakoumelos, A. & Hatzichristou, D. (2008). Presence of a sexual problem may not affect women's satisfaction from their sexual function. *Journal of Sexual Medicine*, 5, 631–639.

Food and Drug Administration. (2015). *FDA briefing document: Joint meeting of the Bone, Reproductive and Urologic Drugs Advisory Committee (BRUDAC) and the Drug Safety and Risk Management (DSaRM) Advisory Committee (NDA 022526)*. Silver Spring, MD: FDA.

Frankl, V. E. (1955). *Man's search for meaning*. New York, NY: Simon & Schuster.

Gallwey, W. T. (1998). *The inner game of golf*. New York, NY: Random House.

Gendlin, E. (1978a). *Focusing*. New York, NY: Bantam Books.

Gendlin, E. (1978b). The body's releasing steps in experiential process. In J. L. Fosshage & P. Olsen (Eds.), *Healing: Implications for psychotherapy* (pp. 323–349). New York, NY: Human Sciences Press.

Gendlin, E. (1996). *Focusing-oriented psychotherapy: A manual of the experiential method*. New York, NY: Guilford Press.

Gottman, J. M. (1999). *The marriage clinic: A scientifically-based marital therapy*. New York, NY: Norton.

Gottman, J. & Silver, N. (2015). *The seven principles for making marriage work*. New York, NY: Harmony Books.

Hart, T. (1997). Transcendental empathy in the therapeutic encounter. *The Humanistic Psychologist, 25*, 245–270.

Hart, T. (1999). The refinement of empathy. *Journal of Humanistic Psychology, 39*, 111–125.

Hart, T. (2000). Deep empathy. In T. Hart, P. L. Nelson & K. Puhakka (Eds.), *Transpersonal knowing: Exploring the horizon of consciousness* (pp. 253–270). New York, NY: SUNY Press.

Irvine, J. M. (2005). *Disorders of desire: Sex and gender in modern American sexology*. Philadelphia, PA: Temple University Press.

Johnson, S. M. (2004). *The practice of emotionally focused couple therapy: Creating connection*. 2nd edition. New York, NY: Brunner-Routledge.

Kaplan, H. S. (1974). *The new sex therapy*. New York, NY: Brunner/Mazel.

King, M., Holt, V., & Nazareth, I. (2007). Women's views of their sexual difficulties: Agreement and disagreement with clinical diagnoses. *Archives of Sexual Behavior, 36*, 281–288.

Kleinplatz, P. J. (1992). The erotic experience and the intent to arouse. *Canadian Journal of Human Sexuality, 1*(3), 133–139.

Kleinplatz, P. J. (1996a). The erotic encounter. *Journal of Humanistic Psychology, 36*(3), 105–123.

Kleinplatz, P. J. (1996b). Transforming sex therapy: Integrating erotic potential. *The Humanistic Psychologist, 24*(2), 190–202.

Kleinplatz, P. J. (2006). Learning from extraordinary lovers: Lessons from the edge. *Journal of Homosexuality, 50*(3/4), 325–348.

Kleinplatz, P. J. (2010). "Desire disorders" or opportunities for optimal erotic intimacy. In S. R. Leiblum (Ed.), *Treating sexual desire disorders: A clinical casebook* (pp. 92–113). New York, NY: Guilford Press.

Kleinplatz, P. J. (2011). Arousal and desire problems: Conceptual, research and clinical considerations or the more things change the more they stay the same. *Sex and Relationship Therapy, 26*(1), 3–15.

Kleinplatz, P. J. (Ed.) (2012). *New directions in sex therapy: Innovations and alternatives*. 2nd edition. New York, NY: Routledge.

Kleinplatz, P. J. (2013). Three decades of sex: Reflections on sexuality and sexology. *Canadian Journal of Human Sexuality, 22*(1), 1–4. doi: 10.3138/cjhs.937

Kleinplatz, P. J. (2016). Optimal erotic intimacy: Lessons from great lovers. In S. Levine, S. Althof & C. Risen (Eds.), *Handbook of Clinical Sexuality for Mental Health Professionals*. 3rd edition (pp. 318–330). New York, NY: Routledge.

Kleinplatz, P. J. (2017). An Existential-Experiential approach to sex therapy. In Z. Peterson (Ed.), *The Wiley handbook of sex therapy* (pp. 218–230). New York, NY: Wiley.

Kleinplatz, P. J. (2018). History of the treatment of female sexual dysfunction(s). *Annual Review of Clinical Psychology, 14*, 29–54.

Kleinplatz, P. J., Charest, M., Paradis, N., Ellis, M. E., Rosen, L., Ménard, A. D. & Ramsay, T. O. (in press). Treatment of low/no sexual desire/frequency using a sexual enhancement group couples therapy approach (2020).

Kleinplatz, P. J. & Ménard, A. D. (2007). Building blocks towards optimal sexuality: Constructing a conceptual model. *Family Journal: Counseling and Therapy for Couples and Families, 15*(1), 72–78.

Kleinplatz, P. J., Ménard, A. D., Paquet, M.-P., Paradis, N., Campbell, M., Zuccarini, D. & Mehak, L. (2009). The components of optimal sexuality: A portrait of "great sex". *Canadian Journal of Human Sexuality*, 18(1–2), 1–13.

Kleinplatz, P. J., Ménard, A. D., Paradis, N., Campbell, M., Dalgliesh, T., Segovia, A. & Davis, K. (2009). From closet to reality: Optimal sexuality among the elderly. *The Irish Psychiatrist*, 10(1), 15–18.

Kleinplatz, P. J., Ménard, A. D., Paradis, N., Campbell, M. & Dalgleish, T. L. (2013). Beyond sexual stereotypes: Revealing group similarities and differences in optimal sexuality. *Canadian Journal of Behavioural Sciences*, 45(3), 250–258.

Kleinplatz, P. J., Paradis, N., Charest, M., Lawless, S., Neufeld, M., Neufeld, R. et al. (2018). From sexual desire discrepancies to desirable sex: Creating the optimal connection. *Journal of Sex and Marital Therapy*, 44(5), 438–449.

Lavie-Ajayi, M. & Joffe, H. (2009). Social representations of female orgasm. *Journal of Health Psychology*, 14(1), 98–107. doi: 10.1177/1359105308097950

Lamb, S., Lustig, K. & Graling, K. (2013). The use and misuse of pleasure in sex education curricula. *Sex Education*, 13(3), 305–318.

Leiblum, S. R. (Ed.) (2010). *Treating sexual desire disorders: A clinical casebook*. New York, NY: Guilford Press.

Mahrer, A. R. (2004). *The complete guide to experiential psychotherapy*. Boulder, CO: Bull Publishing.

Mahrer, A. R. (2008). *The manual of optimal behaviour*. Laval, QC: HG Publications.

Mahrer, A. R. (2009). *The optimal person*. Montreal, Canada: Howard Gontovnick Publications.

Mahrer, A. R. & Boulet, D. B. (2001). How can Experiential Psychotherapy help transform the field of sex therapy? In P. J. Kleinplatz (Ed.), *New directions in sex therapy: Innovations and alternatives* (pp. 234–257). Philadelphia, PA: Brunner-Routledge.

Mahrer, A. R., Boulet, D. B. & Fairweather, D. R. (1994). Beyond empathy: Advances in the clinical theory and methods of empathy. *Clinical Psychology Review*, 14, 183–198.

Mark, K. P., Herbenick, D., Fortenberry, D. J., Sanders, S. & Reece, M. (2014). A psychometric comparison of three scales and single-item measure to assess sexual satisfaction. *The Journal of Sex Research*, 51(2), 159–169.

Maslow, A. (1962). Lessons from the peak experience. *Journal of Humanistic Psychology*, 2, 9–18.

Maslow, A. (1968). *Towards a psychology of being*. 2nd edition. New York, NY: Van Nostrand Reinhold Co.

Maslow, A. (1970). *Motivation and personality*. 2nd edition. New York, NY: Harper & Row.

Masters, W. H. & Johnson, V. E. (1966). *Human sexual response*. Boston, MA: Little, Brown & Co.

Masters, W. H. & Johnson, V. E. (1970). *Human sexual inadequacy*. Boston, MA: Little, Brown & Co.

Masters, W. H. & Johnson, V. E. (1986). *Sex therapy on its twenty-fifth anniversary: Why it survives*. St. Louis, MO: Masters and Johnson Institute.

MacMahon, C. N., Smith, C. J. & Shabsigh, R. (2006). Treating erectile dysfunction when PDE-5 inhibitors fail. *BMJ*, 332, 589–592.

McCarthy, B. & McCarthy, E. (2020). *Rekindling desire: A step-by-step program to help low-sex and no-sex marriages*. New York, NY: Brunner-Routledge.

Meana, M. (2010). Elucidating women's (hetero)sexual desire: Definitional challenges and content expansion. *Journal of Sex Research*, 47(2–3), 104–122.

Ménard, A. D. & Cabrera, C. (2011). "Whatever the approach, Tab B still fits into Slot A": Twenty years of sex scripts in romance novels. *Sexuality & Culture*, 15(3). doi: 10.1007/s12119-011-9092-3

Ménard, A. D. & Kleinplatz, P. K. (2008). 21 moves guaranteed to make his thighs go up in flames: Depictions of "great sex" in popular magazines. *Sexuality & Culture*, 12, 1–20.

Ménard, A. D., Kleinplatz, P. J., Rosen, L., Lawless, S., Paradis, N., Campbell, M. & Huber, J. D. (2015). Individual and relational contributors to optimal sexual experiences in older men and women. *Sexual and Relationship Therapy*, 30(1), 78–93.

Ménard, A. D., Weaver, A. & Cabrera, C. (2019). "There are certain rules one must abide by": Predictors of mortality in slasher films. *Sexuality & Culture*, 23, 621–640. doi: 10.1007/s12119-018-09583-2

Metz, M. E. & McCarthy, B. (2010). *Enduring desire: Your guide to lifelong intimacy*. New York: Routledge.

Metz, M. E. & McCarthy, B. W. (2012). The good enough sex (GES) model: Perspective and clinical applications. In P. J. Kleinplatz (Ed.), *New directions in sex therapy: Innovations and alternatives*. 2nd edition (pp. 213–230). New York, NY: Routledge.

Morin, J. (1995). *The erotic mind: Unlocking the inner sources of sexual passion and fulfillment*. New York, NY: HarperCollins.

Ogden, G. (1999). *Women who love sex*. Boston, MA: Womanspirit Press.

Ogden, G. (2006). *The heart and soul of sex: Making the ISIS connection*. Boston, MA: Trumpeter.

Ogden, G. (2012). *Expanding the practice of sex therapy*. New York, NY: Routledge.

Ortmann, D. and Sprott, R. A. (2013). *Sexual outsiders: Understanding BDSM sexualities and communities*. New York, NY: Rowman & Littlefield.

Perel, E. (2006). *Mating in captivity: Reconciling the erotic and the domestic*. New York, NY: HarperCollins.

Perls, F. S. (1971). *Gestalt therapy verbatim*. Moab, UT: Bantam Books.

Peterson, J. L. & Hyde, J. S. (2010). A meta-analytic review of research on gender differences in sexuality, 1993–2007. *Psychological Bulletin*, 136(1), 21–38.

Plante, R. F. (2006). *Sexualities in context: A social perspective*. Cambridge, MA: Westview Press.

Polkinghorne, D. E. (1989). Phenomenological research methods. In R. S. Valle & S. Halling (Eds.), *Existential-phenomenological perspectives in psychology: Exploring the breadth of human experience* (pp. 41–62). New York, NY: Plenum Press.

Polkinghorne, D. E. (1994). Research methodology in humanistic psychology. In F. Wertz (Ed.), *The Humanistic Movement: Recovering the person in psychology* (pp. 105–128). Lake Forth, FL: Gardner.

Reiss, I. L. (1991). *An end to shame: Shaping our next sexual revolution*. New York, NY: Prometheus Books.

Resnick, S. (1997). *The pleasure zone*. Berkeley, CA: Conari.

Resnick, S. (2012). *The heart of desire: Keys to the pleasures of love*. New York, NY: Wiley.

Rye, B. J. & Meaney, G. J. (2007). The pursuit of sexual pleasure. *Sexuality & Culture*, 11, 28–51. doi: 10.1007/BF02853934

Schnarch, D. (1991). *Constructing the sexual crucible: An integration of sexual and marital therapy*. New York, NY: W. W. Norton.

Schnarch, D. (2000). Desire problems: A systemic perspective. In S. R. Leiblum & R. C. Rosen (Eds.), *Principles and practice of sex therapy*. 3rd edition (pp. 17–56). New York, NY: Guilford Press.

Schnarch, D. (2009). *Passionate marriage: Love, sex, and intimacy in emotionally committed relationships*. New York, NY: Wiley.

Shahbaz, C. and Chirinos, P. (2017). *Becoming a kink aware therapist*. New York, NY: Routledge.

Shaw, J. (2012). Approaching sexual function in relationship: A reward of age and maturity. In P. J. Kleinplatz (Ed.), *New directions in sex therapy: Innovations and alternatives*. 2nd edition (pp. 175–194). New York, NY: Routledge.

Shifren, J. L., Monz, B. U., Russo, P. A., Segreti, A. & Johannes, C. B. (2008). Sexual problems and distress in United States women. *Obstetrics & Gynecology*, 112, 970–977.

Sprott, R. A. & Hadcock, B. B. (2017). Bisexuality, pansexuality, queer identity, and kink identity. *Sexual and Relationship Therapy*, 33(1–2), 214–232. doi: 10.1080/14681994. 2017.1347616

Štulhofer, A., Busko, V. & Brouillard, P. (2010). Development and bicultural validation of the New Sexual Satisfaction Scale, *Journal of Sex Research*, 47(4), 257–268.

Štulhofer, A., Busko, V. & Brouillard, P. (2011). The New Sexual Satisfaction Scale and its short form. In T. D. Fisher, C. M. Davis, W. L. Yarber & S. L. Davis (Eds.), *Handbook of sexuality-related measures*. 3rd edition (pp. 530–532). New York, NY: Routledge.

Traeen, B., Štulhofer, A., Jurin, T. & Hald, G. M. (2018). Seventy-five years old and still going strong: Stability and change in sexual interest and sexual enjoyment in elderly men and women across Europe. *International Journal of Sexual Health*, 30(4), 323–336. doi: 10.1080/19317611.2018.1472704

Twenge, J. M., Ryne A. Sherman, R. A. & Wells, B. E. (2016). Sexual inactivity during young adulthood is more common among U.S. millennials and iGen: Age, period, and cohort effects on having no sexual partners after age 18. *Archives of Sexual Behaviour*, 46, 433–440. doi: 10.1007/s10508–016–0798-z

Van Dam, N. T., van Vugt, M. K., Vago, D. R., Schmalzl, L., Saron, C. D., Olendzki, A. et al. (2018). Mind the hype: A critical evaluation and prescriptive agenda for research on mindfulness and meditation. *Perspectives on Psychological Science*, 13(1), 36–61.

Wolberg, L. R. & Aronson, M. L. (1975). *Group therapy: 1975 – An overview*. New York, NY: Stratton Intercontinental Medical Book Corporation.

Yalom, I. D. & Leszcz, M. (2005). *Theory and practice of group psychotherapy*. New York, NY: Basic Books.

Zilbergeld, B. (1980). Alternatives to couples counseling for sex problems: Group and individual therapy. *Journal of Sex & Marital Therapy*, 6(1), 3–18.

Zilbergeld, B. (1999). *The new male sexuality*. New York, NY: Bantam Books.

Zilbergeld, B. (2004). *Better than ever: Love and sex at midlife*. Norwalk, CT: Crown House.

Index